The
Moneymaker Effect

The
Moneymaker Effect

The Inside Story
of the Tournament
That Forever Changed Poker

Eric Raskin

HUNTINGTON PRESS
Las Vegas, Nevada

The Moneymaker Effect
The Inside Story of the Tournament
That Forever Changed Poker

Published by
    Huntington Press
    3665 Procyon Street
    Las Vegas, Nevada 89103
    Phone: (702) 252-0655
    email: books@huntingtonpress.com

ISBN: 978-1-935396-56-7

Cover Design: Will Tims
Production & Design: Laurie Cabot

Portions of this book were originally published by Grantland.com
and are used with permission.

Dedication

For Olivia and Eli
May they always have both skill and luck
working in their favor.

Acknowledgments

The most logical place to start in thanking people for making this book possible is with the 34 members of the poker community who sat for the interviews that became this oral history. Without their insights, opinions, and behind-the-scenes stories, there would be no book.

Among those 34 interview subjects, there are a handful worth singling out. First, thank you to Chris Moneymaker for his open, honest, and enthusiastic participation across several lengthy sessions. Without Chris' involvement, the whole project would have been a non-starter.

Thank you to Nolan Dalla and Matt Savage for not only their stories and remembrances, but for helping to put me in touch with other interview subjects. Along similar lines, thank you to ESPN.com's Andrew Feldman for facilitating one key interview.

And thank you to Brian Koppelman for both his quotes in the oral history and his astute, lively Foreword. It is an honor to have Brian's byline in my book.

Thank you to my publisher, Anthony Curtis of Huntington Press, for believing in me and this project from the very start. Anthony's perseverance and willingness to be the "bad guy," while allowing me to preserve my "good guy" status, were invaluable throughout the trying process of obtaining the rights to publish my work in book form. Also, thank you to my editor, Deke Castleman, for his hard work and his perceptive suggestions that helped make the final product superior to what I'd originally envisioned.

Backing up a step in the process, I have to thank the folks at Grantland for their guidance and support before I knew I'd be turning this into a book. Thank you to Bill Simmons and Dan Fierman for (a) introducing me to the world of oral history writing, and (b) giving my pitch for a 2003 World Series of Poker oral history article the green light. And a huge thank you to my Grantland editor Rafe Bartholomew, who did a tremendous job tightening up my original article for the site and also was a key advocate for me in my efforts to expand it into a book.

I must thank the people who were instrumental in bringing me into the world of poker journalism in the first place, original *ALL IN* magazine publishers Bhu Srinivasan and Kasey Thompson. A tip of the cap to my long-time partner in poker-mag production Will Tims, without whom I might not have survived in this industry as long as I have, and to Scott Tharler, who was vital in speeding up my poker learning curve. Also, much gratitude to two of the best poker writers I know, Jonathan Grotenstein and Storms Reback, whose WSOP history book made my research on this project considerably easier.

Knowing your subject matter is secondary to knowing how to write and edit, so I must thank my mentors on those fronts, Nigel Collins and Stu Saks. An oral history is primarily an exercise in interviewing and editing, and I learned the ropes of those disciplines under Nigel and Stu's expert guidance.

The most important thank you of all goes to my family, starting with my amazing wife Robin, who put up with a lot of working weekends and even a working vacation, so that

I could complete this book. She did a lot of one-on-two parenting over the past year, and for that I'm extremely grateful.

Thank you to my kids, Olivia and Eli, for motivating, inspiring, and entertaining me. Thank you to my parents, Meryl and Ray, for literally everything, and to Fred, Ari, Dave, Phyllis, Bud, Mark, and too many other people to list for their love and support.

And, finally, thank you to Rodney J. Raskin for giving me an excuse to get out of the house and away from my work for at least a few minutes every day, and for generally keeping his barking to a minimum when I needed to concentrate.

Contents

Foreword

Poker has never been innocent. As long as games have been spread and chips flung across tables, card players have lost fortunes, been cheated, quit in fury, and returned only hours later, ready to bluff off the family farm to some guy named Doc or Red or Dolly.

But there was a time, not too long ago, when there was a charming innocence *about* the game, the professionals who played it for a living, and the amateurs who, once a year, traversed the country to compete against the pros in the World Series of Poker (WSOP) in Las Vegas, Nevada.

This book is about the moment that charming innocence crescendoed before disappearing forever.

Eric Raskin has found the inflection point, the sweet spot, the absolute instant that poker tipped into a cultural obsession, became a giant business, and brought waves and waves of new players into the online poker rooms that turned out, in some cases, to be worldwide criminal enterprises.

Of course, no one knew any of that was in the offing when Chris Moneymaker set out from Nashville for Las Vegas on the freeroll of a lifetime in the summer of 2003. The WSOP tournament organizers did know they'd have a full field, probably the largest in history. They knew that online poker had grown the game and made its rules and rituals accessible to a diverse group of enthusiasts. And they knew that the clash between online specialists and brick-and-mortar regulars could lead to memorable hands, huge swings of fortune, and surprising, dramatic outcomes. But even *they* were amazed by how huge and electrifying it turned out to be.

In *The Moneymaker Effect,* those tournament organizers, along with the railbirds who watched in person and many of the contenders who won or lost at the tables that week, are the ones telling you the story. Which is good news. Poker players sit for long hours, folding, waiting, jawing at one another, and, as a way to avoid falling asleep at the table, many have turned themselves into compelling raconteurs. So what Raskin has done here, turning the storytelling over to the storytellers who were right there in the middle of it, is inspired. I came to this material knowing many of the particulars and still found myself turning the pages quickly and racing to the end.

It's no spoiler to reveal that Chris Moneymaker wins the 2003 World Series of Poker. Anyone interested enough to be reading these words already knows that. Which says something about how big an event this little card tournament became, how prominent a place it has in our collective consciousness.

Moneymaker's victory at the 2003 WSOP was a rapturous moment for Moneymaker most of all, but also for sports fans, poker players, and the poker business. It was also the dividing line between so much that was good about poker and everything that came after.

Eric Raskin's wonderful book puts us there, where we can linger as long as we like as Chris defies the odds, his limitations, and better players—and holds off the uneasy future we know he has to live—in the shadow of poker's most glorious year.

—Brian Koppelman

Introduction

A minute to learn. A lifetime to master. A summer to explode.

The game of no-limit Texas hold 'em has been around since long before anyone was using the words "Tennessee" and "accountant" in a sentence about pivotal moments in poker. But prior to the 21st century, it existed only on the fringes. If your local casino happened to have a poker room, no-limit hold 'em wasn't its most popular game. Now, at many casinos, it's the *only* game spread.

The phrase "all-in" lived many miles outside the common vernacular before—and even for a few years after—we first heard Matt Damon say it in *Rounders*. Now, it's spoken casually even by people who've never played a hand of poker, whether it's your buddy telling you he's "all-in" on the Seattle Seahawks this year or two sitcom characters using the phrase a dozen times over the course of a 23-minute episode to describe their romantic relationship. (That actually happened. The sitcom was "The New Girl," and the episode was titled "All In.")

Poker and popular culture have become intertwined in ways hardly anyone could have imagined. And most of it tracks back to the late spring and summer of 2003, when television, the Internet, and a 27-year-old amateur poker player named Chris Moneymaker all sat down at a table and destiny dealt the cards.

♠ ♠ ♠

Benny Binion wasn't the Texan who brought Texas hold 'em to Las Vegas. That would be Felton "Corky" Mc-Corquodale, a professional poker player from Fort Worth who is credited with introducing the game to Sin City in 1963. (For an explanation of the rules of no-limit Texas hold 'em, see page 235.)

But many years before McCorquodale came to town, Binion did his part to bridge the gap between the wild west mentality of Texas gambling and the bright lights of Vegas.

Binion got into the gaming space as a numbers runner in Dallas. He graduated from there to booking an underground crap game and soon to operating a mobile casino that was reported to have made him as much as a million dollars a year at its peak—not bad money for 1930s America. While pursuing this fruitful, but perhaps less than noble, line of work, Binion showed just how ignoble he could be to protect his business interests, shooting and killing two men (that the history books know of) five years apart. Politically connected and willing to relinquish small pieces of his fortune to maintain his freedom, Binion avoided jail time for both murders.

But in 1946, a new sheriff came to Dallas who couldn't be bought, and Benny moved his family—wife Teddy Jane, sons Jack and Ted, and daughters Barbara, Brenda, and Becky—to southern Nevada. In 1951, he finally entered the above-board (relatively speaking) version of the casino business, buying the El Dorado Club and Apache Hotel on Fremont Street in downtown Vegas and re-inventing them as the Horseshoe Casino. The failing El Dorado needed a makeover, so Binion gave it one, going so far as to spend $18,000 to make it the first property in downtown Las Vegas with carpeting on the casino floor. The Horseshoe offered the world's highest betting limits—and it told you so right outside the entrance, where the sign read, "The World's Highest Limits."

Benny Binion understood the gambling industry and how to employ force to succeed in it, but he also understood the more delicate art of promotion. Toward that end, the year the Horseshoe opened, he organized a publicity stunt that remains legendary within the casino industry more than 60 years later.

Renowned gambler Nick "the Greek" Dandolos told Binion he wanted to be part of the highest-stakes poker game in history and he wanted the Horseshoe to host it. Binion was happy to help—and step one was finding an opponent for Dandolos. Benny knew just whom to call.

Many decades earlier, Binion befriended a fellow paperboy in Dallas named Johnny Moss, who went on to become one of the original Texas "road gamblers," making his living finding juicy cash games stocked with oil tycoons and their modest poker skills. As the cliché goes, it was a hard way to make an easy living. It was also a dangerous way. Moss carried a .38 wherever he went, and he had the hammer removed so he could pull it out of his pocket more quickly. Of all the great Johnny Moss stories—and there are plenty to choose from—the best comes from his wedding night. Johnny was in a poker game and ran out of cash, so he yanked the engagement ring off his bride-to-be's finger and tossed it in the pot. Moss held the winning hand, saving his marriage from ending before it could begin.

Moss happily accepted his old pal Benny's offer in 1951 to come to Vegas and take on Nick the Greek. The two rounders sat at a table strategically positioned at the front of the Horseshoe, where their game attracted deep rows of railbirds throughout its almost nonstop four-month run. Occasionally, other players entered the game—for a minimum buy-in of $10,000. None of them lasted. Finally, Dandolos found himself down an estimated $2 million or $3 million to

Johnny and uttered one of the most iconic phrases in gambling history: "Mr. Moss, I have to let you go."

The biggest winner, other than perhaps Moss, was Benny Binion, who'd attracted extra foot traffic for four months and word of mouth that would last years.

It was 18 years later, in 1969, that Tom Moore, co-owner of the Holiday Casino in Reno, Nevada, hatched an idea he called the Texas Gamblers Reunion, attracting the biggest names and best gamblers in the business to his property for a week. Binion made the trip, along with Moss and such colorfully nicknamed players as Doyle "Texas Dolly" Brunson, Thomas "Amarillo Slim" Preston, Jack "Treetop" Straus, Brian "Sailor" Roberts, Walter "Puggy" Pearson, Rudolph "Minnesota Fats" Wanderone, and Jimmy "the Greek" Snyder. This unprecedented collection of card sharps played mixed games for seven days straight—Texas hold 'em among them—and at the end of event, Binion was suitably impressed to want to rip off the concept.

Inspired by the Texas Gamblers Reunion and remembering the publicity and money he generated nearly two decades earlier hosting the Moss-Dandolos showdown, Binion enlisted Jimmy the Greek's public-relations business to help him invite the world's best poker players to the Horseshoe in May 1970 for the first-ever World Series of Poker.

For days on end, 37 card players battled in a variety of games. When it was over, the competitors were asked to vote for an MVP of sorts, to be named the first poker world champion. After each player received exactly one vote in his own handwriting, they were asked to vote again and this time they weren't allowed to vote for themselves. The 63-year-old Moss, despite being semi-retired from gambling, was the most popular pick, making him the 1970 World Series of Poker champion.

The inaugural WSOP was generally viewed as a success,

but Binion was concerned that it was a bit too unfocused to work as a spectator "sport." Amarillo Slim suggested the idea of a "freezeout"—a competition where every player buys in for the same amount of money and starts with the same amount of chips, and they play until one man has all of them in his stack. In 1971, at the second annual World Series of Poker, seven players bought into the no-limit hold 'em tournament for $5,000 apiece: Moss, Brunson, Preston, Straus, Pearson, Roberts, and Jimmy Casella. Moss won, confirming that his colleagues had voted wisely the year before.

In 1972, the rules remained the same, but the buy-in increased from $5,000 to $10,000. Or at least that's what the public thought. In actuality, each player bought in for $5K and Binion provided the other half, wanting to promote the event as bigger and richer without pricing out any of the competitors. The number of entrants ticked up a notch to eight, and Slim defeated Puggy Pearson heads-up to claim the title.

The next year, the buy-in was a legitimate $10K, and the event was gaining steam. It not only attracted more players (13 this time), but the World Series transformed into an actual series, featuring five tournaments in different disciplines, with the $10K no-limit hold 'em tourney dubbed the Main Event.

The publicity also greatly expanded. Growing into this offbeat novel slice of Americana, the World Series had become an ideal subject for newspaper and magazine articles, as well as the focus of a CBS News documentary narrated by Jimmy the Greek. Puggy Pearson, runner-up the previous two years, won the Main Event in '73 by defeating Moss heads-up, while Moss came back the next year and emerged from a field of 16 players to become a three-time champion.

On the World Series of Poker went, growing at a steady pace, year after year. The legend of Doyle Brunson was cemented in '76 and '77 when he won back-to-back titles, holding a ten and a deuce on the final hand each year. A new guard hit the scene in '78, when a 28-year-old non-Texan college graduate named Bobby Baldwin won the title. In 1980 and '81, a babyfaced Manhattanite named Stuey "the Kid" Ungar won two years in a row, playing an aggressive style decades ahead of its time and earning a lasting reputation as arguably the most naturally gifted no-limit player ever. The first of those two Ungar championships also saw actor Gabe Kaplan reach the final table, helping the World Series blip onto the radar of mainstream news outlets.

In '82, the number of entrants crept into triple digits for the first time, and the enduring dreamer's catchphrase "a chip and a chair" was born when Treetop Straus avoided elimination on a technicality, found himself down to his last chip, and miraculously rallied to win the title.

In '83, Tom McEvoy became the first champion to have won his Main Event seat in a smaller-buy-in "satellite" tournament, shifting the paradigm and making the tournament more open to the everyman than ever before.

Johnny Chan won back-to-back titles in '87 and '88, no small feat against fields of 152 and 167 players, respectively. "The Orient Express" nearly made it a three-peat in '89, only to finish second to Phil Hellmuth, the youngest champ ever at just 24 years old.

In 1991, the field size eclipsed 200 and the top prize reached a million dollars. In '97, when the number of entrants crossed 300 for the first time, a 44-year-old no-longer-baby-faced Ungar beat back his demons and won the title for a third time, wearing sunglasses to try to hide how his nostrils had been destroyed by cocaine.

The next year, a long-haired Vietnamese chatterbox named Scotty Nguyen introduced one of the all-time iconic lines, moving all-in against heads-up opponent Kevin

McBride and warning him, "You call, it's gonna be all over, baby." McBride did, and it was.

When math whiz Chris "Jesus" Ferguson won the Main Event in 2000, more than 500 players entered and the first-place prize hit $1.5 million. Two years later, Robert Varkonyi, a bookish investment banker with a degree from MIT, overcame a field of 631 players to claim the WSOP's first $2 million prize.

For the first 33 years of its existence, the World Series Main Event experienced logical gradual growth, the field size trending upward by a few percentage points each year. After its 34th year, however, all things logical and gradual ceased. That Tennessee accountant, with the prophetic name Chris Moneymaker, won the 2003 World Series and ESPN was there to document it like never before. Poker was just a mouse click away for anyone who wanted to pull up a chair, and the game was never the same again.

The numbers say it all: By 2006, 8,773 players vied for a first-place prize of $12 million.

No-limit hold 'em became a television staple, a pop-culture phenomenon, and a hard way to make an easy living for a generation of brilliant young minds around the globe.

No-limit Texas hold 'em: a minute to learn and a lifetime to master. But not in a million lifetimes could you invent a story as improbable as that of Chris Moneymaker and the summer that gave birth to the poker boom.

Cast of Characters

The subjects quoted in this book were interviewed between August and October 2012, with the exception of Humberto Brenes and Phil Ivey, both of whom were interviewed in July 2013. Below are descriptions of the interview subjects based on who they were and what they'd accomplished entering the 2003 World Series of Poker Main Event. They're listed in the order in which they appear.

Chris Moneymaker

Twenty-seven-year-old comptroller/accountant for three restaurants in Nashville, Tennessee; recreational poker player; married father of a baby daughter.

Brian Koppelman

Co-writer (with David Levien) of the 1998 film *Rounders*, starring Matt Damon and Ed Norton as poker players on the underground New York club scene.

Daniel Negreanu

Charismatic 28-year-old pro from Canada with two WSOP bracelets and an 11th-place run in the 2001 Main Event to his credit; known as "Kid Poker."

Henry Orenstein

Octogenarian Holocaust survivor, inventor, and WSOP bracelet winner; invented the hole-card camera, which was used on American television for the first time in the spring of 2003 on the World Poker Tour.

Cory Zeidman

Florida-based semi-pro high-stakes poker player, specializing in seven-card-stud variants.

John Vorhaus

Author of such poker books as *The Pro Poker Playbook: 223 Ways to Win More Money Playing Poker* and *Killer Poker: Strategy and Tactics for Winning Poker Play*, as well as how-to books on writing.

Jeff Shulman

Poker pro, seventh-place finisher in 2000 WSOP Main Event; *CardPlayer* magazine editor.

Mike Sexton

Veteran poker pro with one WSOP bracelet in his collection; broadcaster for the newly launched World Poker Tour.

Dan Harrington

1995 WSOP Main Event champion and two-time bracelet winner with more than $1.7 million in career tournament earnings; among the notable exports of the legendary Mayfair Club in New York City.

Kenna James

Poker pro, prop player, and former Hollywood Park Casino tournament director who reached his first WSOP final table earlier in the '03 World Series.

Nolan Dalla

Director of public relations for Binion's Horseshoe Casino, beginning in fall 2002; former writer for *CardPlayer* and *Poker Digest*, among other publications.

Annie Duke

Poker pro with 10 WSOP final-table appearances, plus a 10th-place finish in the 2000 Main Event, the second deepest run ever by a woman; younger sister of poker pro Howard Lederer.

Greg Raymer

Connecticut-based patent attorney and part-time poker pro with one WSOP cash on his ledger; known as "Fossilman" for selling fossils to his tablemates as a means of padding his poker bankroll.

Howard Lederer

Veteran poker pro with two WSOP bracelets and two WPT Season One victories to his credit; developed his game at the Mayfair Club in New York; older brother of poker pro Annie Duke; was in the early stages of founding the online site Full Tilt Poker.

Sammy Farha

Houston-based, Lebanese-born, high-stakes poker pro with limited tournament experience, but one WSOP bracelet on his resumé; known for his aggressive style and trademark unlit cigarette in his mouth.

Matt Savage

WSOP tournament director beginning in 2002; co-founder of the Tournament Directors Association.

Lon McEachern

Play-by-play commentator for WSOP broadcasts since the late-'90s; also voiced such off-beat "sports" as billiards and Scrabble.

Barry Greenstein

Poker pro specializing in high-stakes cash games, but with nine WSOP cashes to his credit; gave up a successful career as a founding computer programmer for Symantec to play poker full-time.

Mike Antinoro

Senior coordinating producer for ESPN Original Entertainment.

Bob Chesterman

Senior coordinating producer for ESPN Original Entertainment.

Fred Christenson

Senior director of programming for ESPN.

Matt Maranz

Executive producer for New Jersey-based 441 Productions.

Dave Swartz

Coordinating producer for 441 Productions.

Erik Seidel

Veteran poker pro with six WSOP bracelets and a second-place finish in the 1988 Main Event; former Wall Street trader and regular at the Mayfair Club in New York.

Phil Hellmuth

Nine-time WSOP bracelet winner, including two earlier in the 2003 Series, and the youngest world champion ever when he won the Main Event in 1989; known as the "Poker Brat" for his childish, but often highly entertaining, behavior after losing pots.

Norman Chad

Nationally syndicated sports columnist and author of the book *Hold On, Honey, I'll Take You to the Hospital at Halftime (Confessions of a TV Sports Junkie)*, known for his distinct, humorous, writing style; amateur poker player specializing in mixed games.

Mike Moneymaker

Father of Chris Moneymaker, living a couple of hours away in Knoxville, Tennessee; sports gambling enthusiast.

Dan Goldman

PokerStars vice president of marketing since 2002; marketing manager/director at various companies for two decades prior.

David Gamble

Friend of Chris Moneymaker; founder and vice president of sales for medical supply company ProClaim, Inc.

Lou Diamond

Las Vegas-based professional sports handicapper, once featured on HBO's "Real Sports with Bryant Gumbel."

Peter Alson

New York-based writer, editor, and amateur poker player; author of the book *Confessions of an Ivy League Bookie: A True Tale of Love and the Vig.*

Dutch Boyd

Relatively unknown 23-year-old amateur poker player; prodigy who began attending college at age 12 and graduated from law school at age 18; founder of failed online site PokerSpot.

Phil Ivey

Rising poker superstar with four WSOP bracelet wins already at age 27; nicknamed the "Tiger Woods of Poker" due to his skin color and exceptional talent, though not fond of the nickname.

Humberto Brenes

Costa Rican poker icon, with two WSOP bracelets and 31 cashes on his resumé, including a fourth-place finish in the 1988 Main Event.

Chapter 1

Buildup to the Boom

On Monday, May 11, 1998, a crowd of spectators six or seven rows deep gathered as close to one particular poker table at Binion's Horseshoe as security would allow. It was as if Johnny Moss and Nick the Greek had renewed their rivalry—but Moss had passed away three years earlier and Dandolos three decades earlier, so that couldn't be the explanation.

There was, in fact, one old-school icon from the Moss/Dandolos days at the table: two-time world champion Doyle Brunson. The 64-year-old "Texas Dolly" deserved some small share of the credit for the unusual swarm of onlookers.

But the bulk of the credit belonged to a 27-year-old tablemate: actor Matt Damon.

Damon, who'd won an Oscar a few months earlier for his screenplay for *Good Will Hunting*, was playing in the Main Event of the World Series of Poker as part of a publicity stunt in support of the soon-to-be-released movie *Rounders*.

Across the room at another table sat Damon's co-star, Ed Norton, a Best Supporting Actor nominee for 1996's *Primal Fear* and a fellow emerging Hollywood A-lister.

Damon and Norton had taken poker lessons from the likes of former world champs Phil Hellmuth and Huck Seed to prepare for the Main Event. Neither actor had realistic expectations of winning or even cashing in the tournament. They just wanted to make respectable showings and gin up a little buzz for their forthcoming film.

Norton didn't fare well. About two hours into the tournament, he got knocked out by British pro Surinder Sunar, running his three nines into Sunar's quartet of tens. The reporters and fans who'd been watching Norton quickly migrated to the other movie star in the tourney, jamming the rail around the table shared by Damon and Brunson—for another hour, anyway.

Already somewhat short on chips, Damon got hit with poker's classic cold-deck. He raised with pocket kings and Doyle popped him back with the only superior starting hand, pocket aces. Damon moved all of his chips into the middle, Brunson's bullets held up, and just like that, the *Rounders* boys were both busted.

Their bid to generate publicity in advance of the movie's September '98 release had just as little impact. *Rounders* grossed only $8.5 million in its opening weekend and $22.9 million domestically in all. If not a total box-office bomb (the Miramax picture cost only $12 million to make), *Rounders* was at least a mild disappointment.

Until, that is, it was released on DVD the following February. A tale of two friends battling for their bankrolls on the New York underground poker scene, primarily playing no-limit Texas hold 'em, *Rounders* found its audience in America's living rooms. The highly quotable script by Brian Koppelman and David Levien, the earnest charm of Damon's Mike McDermott, the shady charisma of Norton's Lester "Worm" Murphy, and the confounding accent of John Malkovich's Teddy KGB struck a chord with audiences. It hit heavy rotation on premium cable, then made its way to basic cable. After a slight delay, *Rounders* became a cult classic. And it brought poker considerably closer to the cultural mainstream.

Not all of the characters introduced to America via *Rounders* were fictional. Johnny Chan also became a known quantity, the embodiment of the intimidating poker pro, leading millions of newbies to ask the question, "Wait, people can play poker for a living?"

Along with getting their first glimpse of Chan and his oversized '80s sunglasses, the uninitiated were introduced to the annual competition called the World Series of Poker. Damon's character is seen studying old videotapes of Chan slow-playing a straight and luring Erik Seidel into his trap on the final hand of the 1988 Main Event, securing the second consecutive championship for "Johnny Chan, the master." Chan also plays himself in one brief scene later in the film. As the story goes, Chan shot the scene because his daughter wanted to meet Matt Damon; Johnny had no idea his cameo role would make him, for a few years anyway, the most famous name and face in poker.

That '88 World Series final table at which Chan roped in Seidel, though broadcast at the time on ESPN, predated the use of hole-card cameras. It didn't, however, predate the *idea*. Just a few years earlier, an inventor and poker enthusiast named Henry Orenstein enjoyed a light-bulb moment that forever altered the game.

Orenstein's incredible story very nearly ended before it could begin, as it did for so many Ukrainian Jews at the time of the Holocaust. In 1942, a 19-year-old Orenstein escaped a Nazi death camp when the German guards fled from British and Russian troops. He hid in a ditch, bribed an armed guard to let him scamper across a river, and survived the remaining years of World War II hiding out in a Jewish "kommando" unit of scientists and mathematicians run by German professors, themselves looking to avoid being drafted. Orenstein, ever the odds calculator, later crunched the numbers and estimated his likelihood of surviving the Holocaust at 14,000-to-1.

After that longshot came in, Orenstein made his way to

the U.S. and eventually earned millions (and millions and millions) conceiving a line of action figures called Transformers. His second most famous invention? The hole-card cam.

By positioning small cameras at each seat of a poker table, Orenstein flipped televised poker on its head. His cameras captured an image of the players' hole cards as they lifted the corners an inch off the felt to take a peek. Before the camera, you didn't know what anyone's cards were and poker was boring as hell to watch. You might as well have stared at nine accountants in a boardroom preparing your tax returns. But the information provided by Orenstein's invention changed everything.

The hole cam was used for the first time on American television during the initial season of the World Poker Tour (WPT) on the Travel Channel, which began filming in 2002 and aired in spring 2003. Before that, the list of legitimate poker "celebrities" fit comfortably on one hand: Chan, Amarillo Slim (who'd appeared on "The Tonight Show" several times back in the '70s), and maybe Brunson and Hellmuth. That was about it.

In '03, thanks to the WPT, a few new semi-famous faces were emerging. You had Danish playboy Gus Hansen. You had silver-tongued Brit David "Devilfish" Ulliott. And you had two-time WPT champ Howard "the Professor" Lederer, a graduate of those same New York City underground card rooms where Mike and Worm bluffed their way into and out of danger.

In 2003, poker was beginning to distance itself from that seedy scene and incriminating image. But both were essential to what happened in the years 1998 to 2003, when the foundation for the poker boom was laid.

Chapter 1, focusing on this five-year stretch leading up to the '03 WSOP, features interviews with:

- Henry Orenstein, inventor of the hole-card cam;
- Brian Koppelman, co-writer of the *Rounders* screenplay;
- Nolan Dalla, Binion's Horseshoe public-relations director;
- Matt Savage, WSOP tournament director;
- John Vorhaus, poker journalist and author;
- Lon McEachern, ESPN poker play-by-play announcer;
- poker pros Daniel Negreanu, Jeff Shulman, Dan Harrington, Kenna James, Annie Duke, Howard Lederer, Sammy Farha, and Barry Greenstein;
- semi-pros Greg Raymer and Cory Zeidman;
- poker pro and World Poker Tour broadcaster Mike Sexton;
- and kicking it off, amateur poker player Chris Moneymaker.

"Poker was coming out of the smoky back rooms and into everybody's living room."

Chris Moneymaker: In the late '90s, I used to go to the casinos in Tunica [Mississippi] a lot to bet on sports, play blackjack, whatever. There was a poker room there, but I never went in, because honestly, there were about 15 or 20 guys in there and the average age was about 60, 70 years old, and they looked like they were miserable. So I never even thought to go back there. I stayed out in the pit area.

At the same time, I was playing a little poker in home games. We played Chase the Queen, 357, all kinds of different wild-card games. Around 2000, somebody introduced the game of hold 'em. But it was limit hold 'em and we hated it. This guy had gone to the casino and learned how to play it, but the casino at that time didn't have no-limit hold 'em. All it had was limit hold 'em. We didn't even know no-limit hold 'em was a game, to be honest. It was a couple years later that the movie *Rounders* came out on video. We saw it and we went from playing 357 and Chase the Queen to playing no-limit hold 'em almost exclusively.

Brian Koppelman: I feel that among poker players, and among poker pros in particular, *Rounders* is an important part of a lot of their lives. It clearly wasn't *the* factor in the poker boom, but it was absolutely *a* factor. The beginnings of when the number of people playing hold 'em started to grow and when the casinos started really spreading more hold 'em—there's no question that coincided with when our movie hit DVD and then television.

Daniel Negreanu: Things started feeling different when *Rounders* was released. It sort of created this cult following for poker.

Koppelman: I can't tell you how many times [co-writer] David Levien and I have been walking through a casino and some famous poker player has gotten up and come over to us and said, "Thanks, you guys." That movie brought so many people to the game that it really was financially life-changing for them.

The movie also got it right in terms what it really feels like to play poker. That *was* the cultural touchstone for poker at the time. I think *Rounders* gave people the vernacular and explained the game and what it meant to play Texas hold 'em—what the code was, in a way.

I know when we were writing the movie, all we wanted

was for it to be what *Diner* was for us, a movie that guys, in particular, would quote to each other in their high schools, in their fraternities, in diners. Wherever they were getting together, over a card table, they would quote the movie. And you still can't walk into a card room without hearing, "Pay that man his money."

Moneymaker: I'm pretty sure that watching *Rounders* was the first I'd ever heard of the World Series of Poker. I couldn't name a single poker pro before that. I'd never heard of the World Series before.

Koppelman: The World Series of Poker was so important in writing *Rounders*. I mean, Dave and I watched all those old World Series of Poker broadcasts over and over and over again. And we were always really frustrated there was no hole-card view.

Henry Orenstein: It was about 30 years ago, maybe 1981 or '82. They had a poker show on ESPN and there were six hands in a row where the player didn't call the bet, so we couldn't see what happened! I was sitting there for 10 minutes and I couldn't see anything. It was boring. And then suddenly, the thought struck me that if we put a camera in there, and we were able to see the pros' cards, that that would make the thing much more interesting. So I called my engineers in and within about four weeks, we had a working model. I got the patent around '84, '85.

Cory Zeidman: I think Henry's invention was more important than anything else in taking poker to the next level. Once people were able to see the hole cards, it was like having inside information—seeing who's bluffing, who's not, seeing how quote-unquote easy it is, which it obviously isn't.

Poker became watchable and not totally boring. Those previous World Series of Poker broadcasts of Gabe Kaplan doing commentary with the guy from "Eight Is Enough" [Dick Van Patten], those were torturous! You didn't know who the hell had what. Now it became exciting and interesting.

Koppelman: We had this big argument. In the last poker scene of the movie, Matt Damon's character, Mike McDermott—originally, we'd written it so that you didn't see his cards, so that you didn't know he had the straight against Teddy KGB that mirrored Johnny Chan's straight [against Erik Seidel at the 1988 World Series, a moment Damon's character had studied in *Rounders*].

The director, John Dahl, said to us, "I think we should show the cards."

I said, "No, if you know the cards, it's not going to be as interesting. It's better if you're like the opponent, trying to figure it out."

And John, who was incredibly patient and instructive, and really as curious as we were, said, "Well, let's test both. Let's put them both up in front of an audience. The same exact movie. The only difference in the entire movie is in one version, you can see Matt's cards, and in the other version, you can't see Matt's cards."

We said, "Sure."

But I was certain it would ruin it if you knew that Matt had the winning hand.

So we put it up in front of a crowd. And we played our version, the one where you couldn't see the hand, and it went great. The crowd responded; they were really surprised when the cards turned over. It was awesome.

But when we played the one where you could see that Matt had flopped the straight, the crowd was on the edge of their seats hoping that [John] Malkovich would fall for it.

They were *completely fucking engaged*. Way more engaged. And it was exactly the hole-card phenomenon. They wanted to be inside *Matt's* head too.

John Vorhaus: With the invention of the hole cam, a change took place on the level of storytelling. Now, we're watching a threat unfold where each player in the hand can be thought of as the protagonist of the story.

From a metaphorical point of view, think of a knight in shining armor approaching a cave. We're in the audience; we can see there's a dragon in the cave, but the knight can't see there's a dragon in the cave. This is the way we watch movies.

Now in poker, we can see the dragon, we can see the hole cards, we can see where the threat lies—*Oh, he's about to bluff into a made hand.* We have the omniscience as an audience that we never had before. So suddenly, we can look at poker as an exercise in storytelling. We can watch the story unfold.

ESPN had been broadcasting poker tournaments for years and years without gaining too much traction, because viewers really couldn't know where the threat lay.

Orenstein: The first time somebody used my invention was actually a poker show in England. But the first time in America was the one on the Travel Channel, the World Poker Tour. They paid me royalties. They still pay me royalties.

Jeff Shulman: The poker boom started when the World Poker Tour began airing in the spring of 2003. I remember UltimateBet was literally a day from going out of business. Then once the World Poker Tour popped up, UltimateBet had their ads all over it and everyone wanted to advertise on TV and all the online sites started booming.

Mike Sexton: I don't think the World Poker Tour gets enough credit. Had that show not been as successful as it was in its early days, when it kicked off on national television on a weekly basis, who knows if ESPN would have expanded their coverage of the World Series of Poker? All the networks came on and did poker shows after that, because it was so successful.

And a big factor was that Hollywood got behind poker at that time. We had celebrity shows on the World Poker Tour the first couple seasons, and all the big stars came out and played, and I think because it was so chic and so cool and Hollywood was following it, that really helped the explosion. Ben Affleck was playing, James Woods played, Lou Diamond Phillips played. So you had "Entertainment Tonight," you had "Inside Edition," all these news-magazine shows that were coming out and filming it. It gave it more publicity and a big boost.

Dan Harrington: I remember seeing that the World Poker Tour's ratings and demographics were growing that spring, when every other TV program was falling because of the Iraq War. Everyone was watching the Iraq confrontation on TV. So ratings were down across the board. But not the World Poker Tour. They were gaining viewers.

Kenna James: When I started playing in '96, '97, poker was still in the smoky back rooms. People were ashamed to tell their families that they played poker. They would lie at work; they wouldn't tell anyone that they enjoyed going after work to play a game of poker. There was a still a lot of cigarette smoking at casinos, so these were *literally* smoky back rooms. There was still a lot of cheating going on. But it was slowly growing out of that. And 2003 was the tipping point in which poker was coming out of the smoky back rooms and into everybody's living room. There was a sense that this was something special happening.

Nolan Dalla: As most poker fans know, the World Series of Poker was started by Benny Binion. Benny died in 1989. Just about a decade later, in, I believe, 1998, the entire Binion family split and fell apart. Benny's son Jack took some of the newer properties, for example in Tunica, Mississippi, and Bossier City, Louisiana. The flagship property was Binion's Horseshoe Downtown Las Vegas, and that went to Benny's daughter Becky after the family split. Even though the Horseshoe Downtown was the flagship, the other properties were far more lucrative. And in 1998, no one could foresee that downtown Las Vegas would suffer a horrible slide economically over the next several years. No one saw that coming.

So the family splits. Jack goes off to run his properties elsewhere, and the flagship property goes to Becky Behnen—Becky Binion was her maiden name, then she married Nick Behnen, and Nick was very involved in running the casino, even if he wasn't directly on the property. So Jack was out and Becky was in charge, technically.

Annie Duke: For the older players who'd been playing the World Series when Jack Binion was running the Horseshoe, it was a very big contrast after Becky took over. Under Jack in the '90s—and even more so probably for people who'd been playing in the '80s, but I can only speak directly to the way it was in the '90s—it was this tiny community of people that really looked forward to this big event every year.

Greg Raymer: Benny Binion described the World Series of Poker as a gathering of friends. And it was indeed like that. Almost everybody knew almost everybody.

Duke: Because it was small, the way you were treated was very different. You had a name to everybody working that event. You had access to the top people.

When I first came around, [Tournament Director] Jim Albrecht treated me like he would treat Doyle Brunson, as far as saying hello to me, knowing my name, making sure that I was taken care of. You got comps, you ate free, and I'm not just talking about the snack bar. If you were playing in the tournament, you got comps to the steakhouse. And they used to have this huge buffet upstairs that was legendary. It had, like, alligator meat and all this stuff, and it was looking out on this panoramic view of Las Vegas.

The Horseshoe, at that time, really represented old Las Vegas, the non-corporate version—which obviously had both good and bad things associated with it. But I think in the case of Binion's under Jack Binion, it was really all good. There was a personal touch, and comps weren't dependent on some kind of formula made by some wonk.

Dalla: Becky made some rather poor management decisions regarding the way the World Series was run in 1999, 2000, 2001, and 2002. One of the things she did that was, in retrospect, not wise was she cut back the schedule. She reduced the number of events from more than 20 one year to about 16 the next, because she viewed the tournament as a drain on the resources of the Horseshoe.

This was the first time in history that the number of events was cut, and several top players boycotted the World Series for two or three years, including Doyle Brunson and Dewey Tomko. Doyle had loyalty to Jack Binion and he didn't play at all, not even the Main Event, for two or three years starting in '99.

Duke: When I first started playing the World Series, the rake was tiny. It was 2% on most events and on the Main Event, it was zero. They weren't really looking to make money from the tournaments themselves. It was about the community of players. To everybody who played during that era, the World Series was this incredible convention of your community coming together during this one time of year.

So you had this very nostalgic association with Binion's and what it had been during the Jack years, and as a result, when you came into Binion's in 2003, you had some ambivalence about it. In the '90s, it truly did have this magical feel to it, but by 2003, people felt like Becky was degrading the tournament.

But I guess there was an evolution that had to happen, and you take the good with the bad. I think it's a general parable for the growth of the whole community. When it was a small personal community, the economic opportunity wasn't the same as it was later on. In exchange for this huge boom in the economy, you gave up that feeling of personal connection. There's always going to be a trade-off there.

Howard Lederer: There was a lot of concern about the new people that were running the event and that owned Binion's Horseshoe at the time. There were also ongoing concerns about whether it was going to continue at the Horseshoe. There was never a question as to whether the World Series itself was going to continue *somewhere*, but there were all sorts of rumors about it being sold to another casino. I remember there was talk that MGM, with [1978 world champion] Bobby Baldwin being [CEO of] the Mirage, was looking into buying the World Series. I think I heard he offered $5 million or something like that, which seemed like a lot. When you thought about that, it was like, *Wow, that would be cool, we'd be at the Nugget or we'd be at Bellagio or something.* No one felt like that would hurt the World Series brand in any way. But at the same time, there was an attachment to that physical location, the Horseshoe.

Sammy Farha: I was friends with young Benny Binion [Benny Behnen, Becky's son]. We had a feeling this was going to be the end of the World Series at the Horseshoe. We didn't know where it was going, who was buying it, but we felt that the Horseshoe was weak. But we just were focused on the World Series. It's not our business, you know? Poker player doesn't think about that.

Dalla: I was hired as public-relations director in late 2002 by a fellow named George Fisher, who was the director of poker operations, but he really oversaw a lot more than that. He was probably the most powerful figure at the Horseshoe aside from the Behnens. The 2003 World Series was my first as PR director. It was a bit strange working there that year, because we knew there were offers. There was talk that they were going to sell.

Matt Savage: There was always that behind-the-scenes turmoil: Were they going to pay me? Were they going to pay the dealers? Would there be a revolt? There was always talk about the World Series of Poker not being around anymore. There was always talk about it being sold. There were rumors that they were trying to sell it to a bunch of different people that didn't want it. Obviously, the World Poker Tour was in a great position to buy the World Series of Poker. That seemed like one possibility. But at the time, there was also always talk of it folding, there was always talk of Binion's closing down.

Dalla: At the Horseshoe that year, it was a cross between working in a three-ring circus and being on the Titanic. It was an absolutely wild experience, but it was also a very sad time. You were watching this great thing go down.

We all noticed that they weren't putting any money back into the Horseshoe, and when you see people not putting money into a property, that's the first sign that something's getting ready to happen. If it's your baby, you're going to put money into it.

The Horseshoe had really cool carpeting; it was dark with golden horseshoes in the floor, an elegant-looking carpet when it was laid down in the early '80s. Now it was 20 years old. After 20 years, it had gotten worn down and you had big tears in the carpeting in the high-traffic areas. People could literally trip over the tears, that's how big they were. So the maintenance people started putting silver duct tape over the black carpet. That's how they repaired the holes in the carpet: silver duct tape. That's emblematic of how the Horseshoe was managed and maintained in 2003.

It was sad. It was pathetic. Everyone could see it was going down. We were on the Titanic. This was its last voyage.

Lon McEachern: Part of my job is to convey the atmosphere for the people who are watching, and we didn't have enough hours in the day to talk about what Binion's was really like. On the positive side, you had the history there. To have that Wall of Fame in the back with all the winners and the Hall of Fame members, that just scratched the surface of what poker was all about. On the negative side, Binion's was cramped. The production area was cramped. The hotel rooms upstairs were cramped. And it smelled. You breathed in, you knew you were at Binion's. They did have a good steakhouse up top, though.

Lederer: Binion's Horseshoe was a rundown little hole in the wall, but it was our home.

Side Action _____

Barry Greenstein: I wasn't a tournament player prior to 2003 and I didn't travel to play tournaments at all. I was a cash-game player. Most of the best players were cash-game players at that point.

When the World Poker Tour started, that was the first time the bigger players started thinking, *Hey, I might travel and go to a tournament.*

I'd played in the tournaments in L.A. where I lived, and I'd played in tournaments in Las Vegas, but I'd never traveled anywhere else to play a tournament. And I didn't *really* even go to either of those places for the purpose of playing a tournament. I went there to play the cash games, which were particularly good because of the tournament crowd. Then, as long as I was there, I would play maybe the Main Event of the World Series of Poker or one or two other events at the World Series.

The World Poker Tour started to change that. It led to the high-limit players traveling. We always did it as a group, so we knew there'd be a cash game. We arranged to all go together. And before long, we started playing more tournaments.

Chapter 2

ESPN Antes Up

"For twenty-two years, seven days a week, twenty-four hours a day, Benny Binion's Horseshoe Casino has been called the heart and soul of downtown Las Vegas. Now it's headquarters for the greatest game in town, the World Series of Poker. The defending champ is a gabby guy named Amarillo Slim, who'll walk a mile for a high-stakes action game. And since Binion's is where it's at, that's where Slim is heading to hang his Stetson and defend his title."

These words of narration from executive producer Jimmy "the Greek" Snyder accompany the very first images of the WSOP seen on television, the opening scene of a CBS News documentary on the 1973 Series. It is, by today's standards, and perhaps even by 1973 standards, laughably unwatchable.

The experience of viewing this first attempt at broadcasting the WSOP is not unlike being forced to sit through your grandparents' old home movies, complete with shaky camera work and the constant din of crowd chatter drowning out most of the poorly mic'd table-talk. At 47 minutes without commercials, it's probably 42 minutes longer than it needs to be. Not only can't you see anyone's hole cards, you can't even see the up-cards clearly most of the time; every step of the way, you're relying on Snyder's narration to tell you what's happening. But hey, if extended sequences of players counting out their chips is your idea of entertainment, then this CBS broadcast is for you.

That said, one element of the first World Series of Poker broadcast manages, at times, to reel you in: the players. They're an uncommon breed living uncommon lives, gambling as a means to put food on the table. The average age is about 50. Hardly anyone at the table has a full head of hair. Cigarettes and cigars are fired up mid-hand. It looks like Las Vegas, but it sure sounds like Texas, the laid-back Southern drawls creating the impression that no one's taking the $10,000 buy-in, nor the $130,000 grand prize, all that seriously—even though, of course, they all are.

It's an earlier time and a deeply different culture, populated by colorful personalities speaking a bizarre language that combines the complicated vernacular of poker with a clichéd aphorism for every occasion. "Occasionally, the lamb slaughters the butcher," Slim explains after being eliminated by a runner-runner flush. "Only women and children give up, and I'm neither of those. I'll be back."

As we know now, even if this particular telecast wasn't an artistic triumph, Jimmy the Greek and his partners in production were onto something. Poker's personalities could make for compelling viewing. And so could poker itself. The producers just needed to figure out the right formula.

For the next 30 years, various TV shows made plenty of stabs at it. CBS's "Sports Spectacular" gave it a few tries, as did ABC's "Wide World of Sports." In 1980, ESPN, a fledgling network televising pretty much every sport outside the mainstream, took its first shot at broadcasting the final table of the World Series Main Event as an edited-down one-hour special. ESPN dropped out in '84 and the tournament went untelevised for three years, returning in '87 when ESPN agreed to film not the entire final table, but the play from six contestants down to a champion. The champion that year was Johnny Chan, and as *Rounders* fans know, ESPN remained the TV home of the World Series the following year for Chan's repeat victory. In the late-'90s, the Discovery Channel swooped in for an attempt at broadcasting the World Series, with Steve Lipscomb—who later founded the World Poker Tour—directing.

So it went, with the final table of the Main Event of the World Series of Poker aired in some capacity most, but not all, years from the early '70s through the early '00s. But without hole-card cams, the WSOP on TV never gained real traction. Three decades of trial and error inched the production closer to the pin; by the turn of the millennium, it had improved dramatically over the rookie attempt of 1973. But as of the conclusion of the 2002 WSOP, there was no particular reason to suspect that poker on TV was one or two brilliant decisions away from being perfected—or that the public would watch, even if it was.

As fate would have it, a handful of executives in Bristol, Connecticut, and a couple of producers out of Newark, New Jersey, believed otherwise.

Chapter 2 includes interviews with:

- ESPN Original Entertainment Senior Coordinating Producers Mike Antinoro and Bob Chesterman, and ESPN Senior Director of Programming Fred Christenson;
- 441 Productions Executive Producer Matt Maranz and Coordinating Producer Dave Swartz;
- ESPN on-air poker analyst Norman Chad;
- elite poker pros Phil Hellmuth and Erik Seidel;
- and several characters introduced in Chapter 1, most notably Nolan Dalla, who shares vital insights and memories from his time as Binion's Horseshoe public-relations director.

"Who's ever going to watch poker on TV?"

Mike Antinoro: We were just starting up ESPN Original Entertainment, and [ESPN Executive Vice President of Programming and Production] Mark Shapiro had the idea that we really needed a couple hours one night a week where we could showcase this new programming, build a little bit of awareness about EOE, and get people to see some of the new stuff. I believe it was Tuesday nights.

The first six months, we did a couple of behind the scenes with football teams, a bunch of documentaries. We were looking for something else, something that could draw an audience and fill an hour.

[EOE Executive Producer] Will Staeger took a look at some old ratings reports and saw that reruns of World Series of Poker final tables, these one-hour-long, really poorly produced shows, would pull ratings in the middle of nowhere. They would be like random little blips on the ratings chart. So Will was like, "Why don't we program this in here and see what happens?" And wherever we put poker—and remember, it was old stuff, from two, three, 10 years earlier—it would rate.

So we had a meeting with Shapiro and we discussed it: Why don't we see if there's something we can do with the World Series of Poker now? Old programming, where everybody knows who wins, seems to rate, so why don't we see what we can do with new programming?

Nolan Dalla: The previous World Series of Poker broadcasts were one-hour shows that would appear on the Discovery Channel or ESPN, and they were really basic and rather dull. You cannot encapsulate the excitement and grand theater of the World Series of Poker in one hour, given the incredible cast of characters back then.

Bob Chesterman: It was a very dry production. You saw the hand, and everything happened so quickly, and it was done. There was no setup and you didn't understand anything.

Howard Lederer: I always assumed Binion's Horseshoe was buying time on ESPN. We would get some crappy, no-hole-cards, one-hour thing that would air at like 2 in the morning.

Fred Christenson: I'd been looking at this poker property forever and the production value was just so poor. It just wasn't done in a proper form. We hired some firm out of Vegas in 2001 and 2002 to produce the World Series and they were terrible. I don't even remember the name of them. But the production was a disaster. This outfit out of Vegas, they were nice guys, great guys, but they were just old-school production people and they weren't telling a story.

Lon McEachern: I did the commentary on the final table broadcast in '02. Even though they didn't have a hole-card cam, the producer mounted a full-sized heavy-duty camera underneath the table right next to the dealer, where they put a glass plate in, and the dealer would show each hand to the camera as they folded. Then the producer had to go back and piece together whose cards belonged to what player, and then he brought them up graphically. It was a royal pain in the butt for the producer. But you did have a broadcast with hole cards. Even though the viewer never saw them, the actual card peek, you *did* know what the players had in post-production.

Antinoro: We talked it over with Shapiro and made the decision: Let's go out to Vegas, see the Binion's people, see if we can cut a deal, and see if we can produce it. Obviously, on the programming side and the production side, we didn't want to make this investment, in time or money, for just a one-year deal. We knew we were going to build it into a property, so we didn't want to do it for one year and have someone else take it from us. The thinking was, if we're going to create this franchise here, we need to own it for a little while. So we sent Fred Christenson out to try to make a deal.

Christenson: We'd always done one-year deals with the Binions and it always came down to the last minute. In previous years, we were literally still negotiating with them while the World Series was going on.

So I finally went to Becky Binion in the summer of 2002 and I said, "We need a long-term commitment. We can't do these one-year last-minute deals, because I can't get any money for the production when we do it this way. And the whole key to all of this is the quality of the production. It's never been done in the right way. We need a long-term commitment in order to justify putting the proper money behind the production."

Becky and I went back and forth. Then I went through her husband, Nick—he was actually banned; he could not be on the property at that time. He was a very scary person.

And I would get on the phone with him and I'm like, "We need a long-term commitment." And he wanted a ton of money. And I'm like, "There is no money. The money is all going into the production."

I can remember having a screaming match with him on the phone. I'm like, "You have to give us a long-term deal. Otherwise, it's going to be a shitty production like it has been all the way back to the CBS days."

So we went back and forth and back and forth, and finally he caved. This was in about October of 2002. He said, "All right, we'll do it."

Antinoro: In Vegas, people are gonna definitely watch their back when they're doing business. I think the Binion's people were feeling like, there's an opportunity here. So it's like the Vegas gambling mentality: We gotta get what we can here. We don't want to show our hand too quickly.

Christenson: I never met Becky Binion. The husband, Nick, I've never met him in person either. I only dealt with them on the phone. My understanding was that Nick couldn't legally be on the property in Las Vegas, and Becky, she was a very nice lady, but she was never involved in the day-to-day.

Anyway, we finally got a verbal commitment that fall. But then Becky wouldn't sign the deal. Becky had to sign it and she wouldn't sign. So I went out to Vegas in the spring to get her to sign it. I had a meeting set up and sure enough, she didn't show. I was at Binion's, and Nolan Dalla and two other people were there, and we hashed out a few of the details back and forth, and then they tried to get me to stay at the hotel that night. It was very uncomfortable, the whole thing.

I wouldn't stay there. Nick was kind of out of the loop at this point, but you could feel his presence. Everybody had their marching orders and they were just trying to squeeze money out of us. And again I'm like, "*There is no money.* The money is all going into the production."

Becky finally signed the deal in the spring of 2003. It was a five-year deal. They ultimately did get some money, but it was under six figures—I think it was $80,000 a year; it wasn't much. But the pitch to them was, "We're going to show the world what you have here, like it's never been shown before, and they will come." For them, it was about the promotion for their casino and their business. We were going to pump a lot of money into the production and this was going to be the greatest marketing tool in the world.

Chesterman: Prior to 2003, we hired a third party to do the production and we were just airing the shows. For 2003, we took production up internally. I acted as executive producer and ran all the money and hired Matt Maranz and 441 Productions. I'd worked with them previously at NBC doing the Olympics and these guys are great, great storytellers. So we hired them, and Matt and Dave [Swartz] oversaw the day-to-day responsibilities and I managed the budget and the whole project.

Matt Maranz: I had done a lot of documentaries for ESPN in the past and I'd been pitching poker and the World Series of Poker as a documentary, probably beginning in like 2000 or 2001. And they always turned it down. I'd go in there with six or seven ideas, and I'd throw in poker as well. And they would turn it down, saying, "Who's ever going to watch poker on TV?" That type of remark.

Then in 2003, they finally said, "Yes, let's give it a try."

But what I was pitching was a documentary. They had a different idea. What I was pitching is not the World Series as you know it.

Chesterman: If Matt had pitched it to ESPN before that, I don't remember it. I remember us approaching them on it. I'd always wanted to work with them on a project and this was the perfect project for them.

Maranz: It was probably February when we started talking about it. Back then, the World Series was in May; it ended the week before Memorial Day. So once we decided to do it, we had to hurry up and learn about poker.

I had zero poker knowledge prior to this. I'm not a poker player. I never played poker before, outside of maybe one night in my dorm room with some friends. But I read a book called *Big Deal* by Tony Holden, a British author, and it was about the life of a professional poker player. What I was intrigued by were the characters—the people who decided they were going to play poker for an occupation. That struck me as an interesting career choice back then. The characters and the stories appealed to me, but I knew nothing about the game.

So we went out to Vegas as quickly as possible to learn about poker. From April through the whole early part of the World Series, I was out there meeting poker players and learning about them. I did a lot of reporting and research in that one month leading up to the Main Event.

Dave Swartz: When we walked into Binion's for the first time to get a sense of the game and how everything was played, we were immediately struck by, *Wow, this is a really interesting group of people.* Poker had this stereotype. It had this stereotype of back-room games, cigar smoke, maybe some seediness to it. And that's not what we found at all.

What we found was a group of really interesting people and *incredibly* intelligent people. When we sat down to interview people, we knew right away, *Wow, we have met our match!*

These are people who have a lot to say on a wide variety of subjects, and who think about a game on a level no one realized you think about at the time. That was all new at the time and something that we found really interesting—the way these guys approach the game from a strategic and mathematical standpoint.

It was a battle, a man-on-man battle, a battle of the mind, a battle of personality. A cognitive battle. It was a really interesting game played by these incredibly interesting characters. These were people that I wanted to get to know more about, and once you sit there as a producer and say, "I want to know more about these people," you kind of think and hope that the viewers will say that too.

Dalla: "Eccentric" is a good word to describe most poker players of that era and before. Just the fact that you'd pay $10,000 to play in a poker tournament makes you a little different than the average person on the street.

Antinoro: Seeing these guys in person, it was almost like watching a western movie. These are some real characters here, and they're not acting. They're themselves. This is who they are.

Maranz: There's a saying that the only thing more interesting than a poker player is the person sitting next to them. It was a unique breed of person who decided to become a professional poker player. They came from all walks of life, they all were incredibly smart in unique ways, and they all had an interesting story to tell of how they got to that seat. And we were confident that was going to resonate.

Dalla: So it's the spring of 2003, there's standard preparations for the World Series, and George Fisher comes in to me one day and he says, "By the way, we're going to have ESPN film the World Series this year."

I didn't have any idea how big this moment was going to be for poker. But I knew it was important, in that the world's premier sporting network was going to come in and make a major investment in time and resources.

So George Fisher says, "You're going to be handling all that."

And I'm thinking, *Well, I'm not making that much money, and you're basically saying I'm going to do double the work now? Not only do I do all the reporting and the writing and the overnight chip counts and the administration, but now I'm going to be responsible for the TV element?* I rolled my eyes; I wasn't particularly happy with this additional workload, not realizing just how important this moment was going to be.

Matt Savage: The guys from 441 Productions came in as green as could be, asking me questions like what hand beats what hand, what the slang in poker is, and all that. They did their homework and did a good job that first year, but it was a big transition. It was a lot of extra work for them and for us.

Dalla: As far as the added workload for me, keep in mind that there was no research team. We didn't have a lot of statistics at the time, other than how many gold bracelets somebody has won. We didn't have a great database regarding accomplishments and things that are really important in terms of telling a story.

ESPN shows up, and with all due respect to them, they don't know anything. So they're asking for an enormous amount of background material: Who's the oldest to do this? Who's the youngest to do this? Is this the first time this has ever happened?

These questions, whenever you hear Norman Chad or Lon McEachern delivering a line, that line may have taken an hour to research. Nowadays, we have a great database and we can pull a lot of this stuff up; at the time, we didn't have it. So a lot of research involved picking up the phone and calling Doyle Brunson and asking him, "Doyle, do you remember in 1993 when …" That was our research. It didn't come across on TV how much research was required to do one of these shows.

Don't get me wrong. It was a great privilege to be a part of all this and work with the media that were there that year, but it was a shitload of work. It was 24 hours a day. You were constantly being bombarded with tasks.

Maranz: We had to learn the game, and tournament poker is different than regular poker. We had no idea that poker tournaments go on *forever*. These guys are playing 12, 15, 16 hours a day. An NBA game is three hours.

So the first thought was, *Do we make them change the game and play it under a more TV-friendly format?*

But poker was different from the NBA or the PGA, in that these guys were putting up their own money to play. They weren't being paid to play, they were *paying* to play. So I felt they had a stake in the say of all this and I decided we weren't going to change anything. We were going to approach it like this event was existing, and we were going to come in and cover it.

We let them play as long as they wanted to play. We never tried to change the structures or anything like that. We kept the integrity. That was really our first big decision: *You guys do what you do, and we're just going to chronicle it.*

There were many 4 a.m. and 5 a.m. nights, though, when I was like, *That was the stupidest decision I ever made.* But it was the right decision.

Lederer: I remember talking to Matt. He was very new to the game and he asked me what I thought about a TV table. His initial idea was, "Well, maybe they can rig it so there will be a lot of big names at the TV table."

And I said, "No, you can't do that. What you can do is you can select the table that looks best to film and then move those people over."

But even that was a little controversial. The idea that you're going to have a tournament that has 80 tables, and one of those tables is going to be a featured table with hole-card cams, there were concerns that that might affect the game. One table is going to be having a different experience than everyone else in the tournament. People were talking about that from a game-integrity perspective.

Maranz: Howard was instrumental in teaching me about poker and players. As was Annie. Phil Hellmuth was instrumental, Erik Seidel was instrumental, Chris Ferguson was instrumental. That was the core group, the first core group that really allowed me access to the world and talked to me about poker and ways to cover it.

Chesterman: When Matt and Dave made the connections with the players and everybody understood that we were really putting our time and effort into this project, we started to gain the trust of everybody. And that's important, because in the end, when you're going to look at everybody's cards, you need a lot of trust. That was the biggest hurdle to overcome, us being able to see their cards and them getting comfortable with that.

Savage: Erik Seidel was very vocal about not wanting to use the hole-card cameras. He didn't want anything to do with it. I recall Erik speaking up about how it was going to change the game, ruin the game, give away too much information about how he plays.

Swartz: Actually, a lot of players weren't into it and

didn't want to show cards. Erik Seidel is the one who really stands out in my memory. Erik couldn't have been more helpful in terms of coverage and characters and helping us learn the game, but he didn't want us to see his cards. It was new, it was different, and people were worried it was going to change the game.

Lederer: Erik was reluctant. He is one of my dearest and longest friends, I've known him for 30 years, and he is one of the best guys in poker. And he's a games player. He was a world-class backgammon player; he was a very successful trader on Wall Street. He's a very close friend—and he has helped me less than just about any of my friends in terms of sharing strategies and talking about poker. He likes to keep his strategies to himself. That's just who he is.

So probably more than any other pro I know, the idea of showing his hole cards to the whole world really affected him.

Erik played like crap on every TV table that he played at for a long time. He didn't want to show the world how he played. So it did take him awhile to embrace it. But he got it—he understood what it would mean to the game. He never lobbied against it. It just really affected him.

Erik Seidel: I personally didn't feel comfortable playing with hole-card cameras, but some of it also was about the fact that we weren't getting compensated for it. It seemed weird to me that in every other major sport, when people are on TV, they're compensated and they're compensated well, whereas here we were on TV, essentially teaching other people how to beat us—teaching other people how we play and giving out information that's very valuable to people—but there was no compensation. So that was part of it.

But the other part of it was just my discomfort. I've never

been used to people seeing what I'm doing, and even to this day I'm uncomfortable with it.

Savage: We consciously decided not to move Erik to the featured table, because he said that he would hide his cards.

Seidel: I remember they asked me Day One if I would be at the feature table, and I said I preferred not to. And I remember thinking about that and wondering, *Well, did I make a mistake?* This was the beginning of poker on TV and obviously, there would be some value to getting your name out. But I'm such a purist in a sense that I just wanted to play and I didn't want to think about anything else besides the hand. I was self-conscious about what I might be doing.

But I certainly wasn't like, "These people should be banned. Why are they showing hole cards?"

I knew it was good for the growth of the game—in fact, I wrote an article about how this was going to change the future of poker.

Dalla: The mechanics of the hole-card cams were difficult. They used cameras that weren't part of the table the way they are now. Back then, there were wires all over.

Swartz: Look back at the table from the 2003 World Series and you'll see what we did. We took these tiny cameras and wrapped green felt around them and laid them on the table. Those were the hole cameras. They weren't built into the table. We took an existing poker table and we jimmy-rigged it to put these cameras on the table, wrapped with felt, so hopefully the viewers wouldn't see them.

Dalla: Players would show their cards, but wouldn't be positioned in front of the camera properly. So they'd be asked to move over two inches. Or, "Can you be sure and show your cards longer?" Staff would have to go up all the time and remind players of the procedures.

So this was a little bit … I don't want to say annoying, but if you're at the featured table at the World Series of Poker, you don't want to be tapped on the shoulder every five minutes, reminded to do these things.

Still, I didn't really hear any complaints about it. Most people understood that this was part of a greater good for the game.

Annie Duke: I was very stiff in my assessment that nobody would ever want to watch poker on television. I was completely wrong, by the way. I'm not a visionary. I just couldn't imagine that watching a bunch of people play poker would grab anybody's interest. I couldn't really see what the impact of the hole-card cameras would be and how much it would wake up this population of people who were playing poker at home. So, I'm an idiot.

I don't get the pet rock either.

Swartz: A major question was how to cover this. Our background was more in documentaries than features, but Matt and I had both worked in and around live sports television for a long time. So while I think we might have originally gone into it with more of a documentary perspective when the idea originally germinated, we quickly adapted our own live sports mentality in terms of the coverage.

I can remember sitting in meetings with the EOE team— me, Matt, Chesterman, Mike Antinoro, and some of the other producers who were brought on to do the series—fleshing things out and realizing that we had to take a whole new approach to the coverage, because it was unlike anything that was out there in sports television or documentary television. It had to be kind of a combination of the two.

Maranz: It was a hybrid. It could not be a straight documentary, where you wanted to follow one or two or three players. You actually were following an event. So it was basically a documentary feel toward a live sporting event. We tried to meld those two together. It's character-driven sports coverage.

Chesterman: You didn't want to alienate the true poker fan, but you also wanted to bring in new poker fans. So you needed to walk the fine line of storytelling, without pushing people away with too much storytelling.

Phil Hellmuth: I think Matt Maranz is a genius. He brought personality into poker. The World Poker Tour brought cards. But Matt Maranz brought personality.

Maranz: The World Series of Poker had been on for 20, 30 years before that, just the final table. A one-hour show or two-hour show of the final table. But the people on the programming side wanted more this time. They wanted to make as many shows as possible out of this. That's a business model in TV: You set up once and shoot as much as possible, while you can.

Chesterman: When you can get some multiple amount of programming from one production setup, economics always comes into it.

Maranz: As we did our research and we thought about how to produce this, we realized that it wasn't just the final table. They played for four days prior to that and you could actually create a lot of programming from the earlier days of the contest.

In some regards, the earlier part of the competition is more interesting. At the final table, you only have the nine guys who made it there. It's a crapshoot who makes it there. But all the famous players and stars and personalities are there on Day One, and you can actually showcase them and build arcs and storylines to get to the final table.

So I think it started with the programming initiative, the question of how do we create more programming. Then we took over on the storytelling side, realizing there's a great opportunity to start as early as possible in the tournament and build these characters.

Dalla: This had never been done before. They filmed, essentially, the story of the Main Event from Day One.

Swartz: I remember a couple of things that were complicated in figuring out the right production strategy.

One was how to present individual hands: the question of how we're going to cover this from a camera perspective. When you watch the pace of the game, it's incredibly fast. Cards are dealt, everybody acts, hand's over, and you're like, *Whoa, how can you possibly make this into compelling television?* I vividly remember thinking, *How are we going to slow the pace down on television, so we can talk about what the individual moves in hands mean? How are we going to break this down so that viewers find it interesting?* Because at the time, viewers didn't know the game. We had to take each individual hand and make it presentable for people who had never seen, watched, thought about, or cared about poker ever before.

We approached the shooting of it in a very cinematic

way. From a lighting perspective, from a camera-blocking perspective, and from a camera-coverage perspective, the approach was let's get in there, let's get tight on every face, let's move from the cards up to the face.

The second big strategy was coming up with this concept of the feature table and the field. I compared it a little bit to tennis coverage, that you're going to have your main match on Center Court, but every now and then you're going to bounce out and cover what's happening on Court 2, Court 16, so that you give people a sense of what's happening in the overall tournament. And that became the model for that first year of coverage, and it has continued to be the model to this day.

We might have come in thinking we'd cover five tables at once. But once you see the game and how it's played, you realize one camera can't fully cover a hand and you need to block things out, so you're providing full coverage at one main table. And then at the outer tables, you get a sense of what's going on in the rest of the tournament, and that's also where you meet the characters who will eventually become important throughout the tournament.

Maranz: I was the one who recommended who to hire on the talent side. Norman in particular was interesting, in that he was friends with the other guys from ESPN, the Mark Shapiros and Mike Antinoros, and he'd worked with them before.

Norman Chad: I had done a little on-air work for ESPN and also was a consultant, because I knew Mark Shapiro, who was rising up the ranks at ESPN. On air, I had done mostly sportswriter stuff, like "PTI." And I had done some stuff on ESPN Classic. I was the co-host of "Reel Classics," and for a while they did a version of "The Sports Reporters" on ESPN

Classic, called "Classic Sports Reporters." So those were the couple of things I had done. But I had never done color commentary like this before. I had virtually no TV experience.

Maranz: I knew Norman as a sports columnist. Norman was a huge gambling fan. So when we started doing this, Mike Antinoro suggested I talk to Norman, just to learn about poker a little bit.

Chad: Mark Shapiro had me consulting with 441, because they had no poker experience, and as I used to tell it, I was the only person Mark knew with a gambling problem. He knew that I went into a poker room from time to time. So I was consulting with them for several months, through conference calls and emails and the like.

Maranz: I would talk to Norman. "Tell me who's an interesting character, how you play the game," things like that. And eventually I realized, *Wow, he actually could be an excellent broadcaster of poker*. So I started talking to Norman about it. I gave him some hypothetical about what we would be looking for in an announcer and I started skewing the conversation toward things that Norman did. He had no idea what I was asking, that I was saying, "You would be good at this."

Eventually, he figured it out. And he said, "Wow, I guess you're talking about me."

Chad: I wish I remembered that, but I don't.

I know Matt called me one day, and this is the part I don't remember that well. I thought he just called me out of the blue and asked me, do I have any interest, had I ever considered doing poker commentary on TV?

I remember thinking, *Geez, what kid from the time he was*

six years old doesn't dream of doing poker commentary on TV? But I remember him telling me that they'd decided it was best to go without a poker player for several reasons and that when they were dealing with me in the various ways over the last several months, either by email or by phone, I seemed to have the qualities they might want. So he asked, "Would you like to do it?"

I told him I'd get back to him.

I really didn't know if I was going to do it. I remember bringing it up with my closest friend later in the week and he said, "Why wouldn't you do it?"

I said, "Well, I don't know, it's just poker, and I've got other stuff to do."

And he went, "What other stuff to do? You have no career right now."

I said, "That's a pretty good point."

It didn't seem like that big of a deal, though. It was poker on television. They'd never done more than an hour or two of it per year before and it didn't seem like it was a life-changing event. It was just something I was going to do for the next year and see how it fit.

So I called Matt back and said, "Sure, I'll do it."

Antinoro: I'm not going to call Norman the Howard Cosell of poker, but it's close. He made the telecasts interesting. Lon was the perfect straight man, and Norm presented the game in a way that, I think, was a big, big key to the success of the broadcasts. He had a little bit of a polarizing personality for poker fans, which I think is huge. Not to go crazy, but "Monday Night Football" doesn't become "Monday Night Football" without Howard Cosell. And I don't think the World Series of Poker becomes what it became without Norman Chad.

Chesterman: Norm is polarizing. Internally at ESPN, not everyone loved that decision. But I certainly did.

Maranz: Back then, there weren't enough people playing poker, among viewers, who really understood the game. So to go with a straightforward, hardcore, Xs-and-Os poker pro probably wasn't going to work. The viewers needed to be entertained.

It was a show about poker. Not necessarily a poker show.

Norman understood the game enough and obviously, he's an entertaining guy. Some people love him, some people hate him, but most people listen to him, which is what you want in an announcer.

Swartz: I certainly remember discussions about whether Norman was the right fit for this type of thing. Lon had called poker before. But Norman was a gamble.

I remember the first time we were voicing with him. Normally, when you're doing a football game, it's "Hi, I'm Al Michaels, alongside longtime coach John Madden" or "alongside former wide receiver Cris Collinsworth." Norman was not known like that, so we almost had to set him up, let the viewers know that he indeed had some expertise. I think if you go back to that first show, we might have called him "tournament poker player Norman Chad."

But it wasn't his poker expertise that made him stand out, in my opinion. It was his poker sense, along with his common sense, and obviously his sensibility in terms of humor and just putting everything into perspective, that not only made Norman work, but really helped make the show work, the series work, that year and for many years to come. He was a huge part of all of this.

Maranz: Lon came in after we had Norman signed up.

We were looking for a play-by-play guy, and frankly there weren't too many of them who had any poker experience. And Lon's a professional broadcaster. He'd done lots of sports before, lots of more obscure sports, and he'd done the World Series before.

McEachern: I had done a lot of stuff for ESPN; it was always one-off events, do an event here, do an event there. I was just trying to make a living as a freelance sportscaster, never under contract, never a full-time employee of ESPN. I was just a hired gun. And because I knew a producer who knew a producer, the way things go, I was hired to do some poker.

Then, as it happened, when 9/11 hit, all jobs in the world contracted and a lot of shows that ESPN would have given to freelancers such as myself, they had to give to their staff people. So I lost a lot of work as a fallout of all that. And I was hurting. I was unemployed for like 18 months.

I had a friend in the banking business, and I went into banking, actually, as a loan officer. I kept trying to dabble in TV and kept thinking I could make it, but with a family and a mortgage, it was very difficult. So I took up this guy's offer to be a loan officer for a Washington Mutual bank in Sunnyvale, California, and it was fine doing that. It was perfect timing for me. It was the housing boom, rate finance frenzy. I look back on those years very often, because it was just the choice I had to make at the time to give up broadcasting, and I had faith that if I gave it up and it was the right thing to do, it would come back.

Sitting at my desk one day, I got a phone call from a producer at ESPN. I had no idea how he got my number. He said, "We saw you did the '02 World Series, and we're going to be doing some shows from this year's World Series, and we're wondering if you could do it." It was totally out of the blue.

I hadn't had any contact with him, and I had to call him back later, because I had to check my vacation schedule to see if I had enough time off at the bank to get away for the shows. Luckily, I did.

I wasn't there for the whole Main Event. I got there late because I had to work, but I managed to squeeze it in and to squeeze all my vacation out to do the voiceover work that we did in New York. It was going to be seven one-hour shows and at that point, it was money that I needed, just a job. I didn't know what I was getting into.

When it was over, I kept working at the bank. I stayed with them until '05, juggling both, until finally we just started doing too many shows and I couldn't do both. I couldn't service my customers. So I gave up the bank.

But when I did finally sign a contract for a three-year deal with ESPN, there was language written into it that I had an out—if the banking business was what I decided I wanted to do, I could leave the shows and do that.

Chad: I'd never met Lon before. I don't think there's ever instant chemistry with me. I'm an acquired taste. Most people don't really get along with me at first.

But Lon and I, we pretty much clicked early on. Lon's much easier to get along with than I am, so there were no real potholes on the road at the beginning. It pretty much was hand in glove.

McEachern: This was my first time meeting Norman, but I'd been a fan of his column. He had an NFL-picks column that was syndicated in the *San Jose Mercury*, so I knew his work and would laugh out loud at his stuff. I really clicked with what he wrote. So it was a thrill to meet him.

It was amazing how we clicked early on and just got

along. The stuff I needed to do worked well with what he needed to do. We didn't cross each other's paths and we talked a lot about the game.

Christenson: The last major hurdle was that we had to get the approval of Nevada gaming to use the hole-card cameras. As a last-minute thing, they were telling us we couldn't use them. I think Nolan Dalla and those guys at Binion's signed off on it, but Gaming Control had to come in and make sure the security was right.

Maranz: There was huge resistance to putting hole cameras in the table, to the point that it almost didn't happen. To the point that ESPN even backed down and said, "Okay, we won't do hole cameras." Myself, I was like, "That's not a good decision. We really need hole cameras on this."

Chesterman: You had everybody at the Gaming Commission very uneasy and we were like, "What do we need to do to gain your trust?" I was actually positioning a guard with a shotgun right outside the area where the video feeds were, and we said only two people are allowed to go in this area. Nobody else was allowed in there at all. Like it was a sanctuary.

So that's what we landed on, a guy with a shotgun standing there, in front of a bunch of black curtains securing this one area.

Maranz: Phil Hellmuth, actually, was a huge help in this. People like or hate Phil, but he took it upon himself to approach Binion's and to really convince them to allow hole cameras. Without that, I don't think there would have been hole cameras.

He went to them and said, "There will never be a poker tournament on Earth that doesn't have hole cameras. So you can either be ahead or behind."

Phil always thought of it very big picture. He was instrumental in this.

Antinoro: We communicated to the Binion's people and the Nevada people that this wasn't a live event.

Look, I understood their concern. There's an incredible amount of money at stake. Obviously, there's a lot of ways that people we hired and didn't have control over could take advantage of the hole cameras. I think that was their biggest concern.

But they also knew that good things would come from having this on ESPN, so ultimately that's really what won out.

I'm not sure anything we did or showed them alleviated their fears. It was more a matter of making it clear that we were only going to do it with the hole cam, so they didn't have any choice.

Chesterman: We couldn't just pack up and leave, so as I remember it, we were at the point where we were making a decision to do this without the hole cameras. Luckily, we were able to convince them by (a) getting the comfort level with us and (b) pulling out the guy with the shotgun.

I think we got it resolved just one day before the Main Event started. It was too close for comfort.

Side Action _____

Lon McEachern: I was in Las Vegas a few years ago, playing a small cash game somewhere, and I got to talking with some older guy across the way. He told me that he'd been in Las Vegas during the '03 Main Event, and he'd been asked by some guys to come upstairs at Binion's and meet with some people.

He went to one of the rooms in the hotel, sat down, and was told about an investment opportunity. They were telling him it was an investment opportunity unlike any other, and they were asking for $100,000—which he said he had. And he turned them down.

He walked away from Howard Lederer and Chris Ferguson and others who were starting Full Tilt Poker.

So you had the beginning of the poker boom and the beginning of the online poker boom really happening at the same time, in the same building, on different floors. This guy probably regretted that decision for a while, but who knows, by turning them down, he might have saved himself from ending up in jail.

Chapter 3

The Chris Moneymaker Story

Maybe you had an Internet connection in your home; maybe you didn't. Maybe you had an email account; maybe you didn't. Maybe you had a cell phone; maybe you didn't.

As of January 1, 1998, the technology that we now can't live without was just beginning to get its hooks into us. And on that date, New Year's Day of '98, a company called PlanetPoker dangled the hook every poker enthusiast eventually bit on: real-money online poker.

Because of slow Internet connections (remember that awful screech of your dial-up modem connecting?), because most people were still uncomfortable paying for anything online, and because no one had yet thought about using the words "poker" and "boom" in the same sentence, PlanetPoker was not an instant sensation. But it was a pioneer and a game-changer, and other sites soon followed: UltimateBet, ParadisePoker, PartyPoker, PokerStars.

Online poker offered numerous advantages that live casinos couldn't match. Thanks to minimal overhead—no dealers to pay, no actual cards, chips, or tables required—a poker site could charge a smaller rake than a brick-and-mortar casino. You want to play a $60 tournament at a casino? Be prepared to pay $75 or $80 with the house's entry fee figured in. You want to play a $60 tournament online? You're probably talking about $3-$5 for the house.

Then there's the convenience. You can fire up an online

poker game any time of day, spur of the moment, no travel time required, no gas, tolls, or parking. If you have even a five-minute window, you can sit down in a ring game, play a couple of hands, and cash out.

In an online game, there's no guesstimating about opponents' chip stacks, because the exact numbers are right in front of you at all times. There are more game options than any casino can offer: cash games, multi-table tournaments, sit-and-go's, and satellites at just about every price point imaginable.

There's no cigarette or cigar smoke (unless you want there to be), no random dude's body odor, no drunk guy who won't shut up.

And, of course, you can play in your underwear.

Perhaps most importantly—yes, more important even than the underwear factor—the game moves considerably faster online. There's no time spent shuffling and dealing cards or counting out chips. It's been estimated that an online table sees about four times as many hands per hour as a casino table—and that's before you consider "multi-tabling," the opportunity to spread several games across your computer monitor at once.

Online poker wasn't just an alternative way to enjoy the game. It was also a way to learn on a dramatically accelerated curve, to experience as many hands in 12 months as Doyle Brunson had in his entire life. It not only brought millions of new players into poker; it forced those who had been playing all their lives to adjust and evolve or risk being left behind.

Long before Chris Moneymaker discovered poker, live or online, he'd been indoctrinated into the world of gambling by the same man who gave him his famous surname: his dad, Mike. The elder Mr. Moneymaker exposed his son to blackjack and sports betting at a young age—always preaching responsible gambling, but not always finding an attentive audience for that sermon.

Chris remained close with his dad when he "left" for college—not just in the emotional sense, but physically as well. Chris was a student at the University of Tennessee, where Mike ran the campus motor pool.

Chris attended his share of classes and studied for most of his exams, but nothing commanded his attention at UT quite like drinking and gambling. Sports betting was his primary vice, and Chris and Mike even shared a bookie and a bankroll.

Chris juggled his extracurricular activities with his studies successfully enough to graduate. He then earned his masters in accounting, also from Tennessee. Living with his girlfriend Kelly, Chris couldn't quite rise above the post-graduate-school paycheck-to-paycheck lifestyle, forever trying to dig his way out of credit-card debt and pay off college loans, occasionally borrowing money from his parents along the way.

Chris and Kelly got married and soon their money troubles worsened: He lost his job with Deloitte & Touche in a round of layoffs shortly after 9/11 and found himself not only borrowing money from his parents, but from his close friend Bruce Peery, as well.

Fortunately, Chris wasn't unemployed long. He got a new job early in 2002 as a comptroller/accountant for three Nashville-area restaurants. But he was making a considerably smaller salary than he had been at Deloitte, only $32,000 a year—not enough for a married man expecting his first baby in the spring of 2003, especially one with loans and debts constantly hounding him.

For 27-year-old Chris Moneymaker, the everyman struggling every day to provide for himself and his growing family, online poker was a welcome diversion and a way to periodically supplement his income. He never planned for it to be anything more than that. But in the Internet age, a change of plans is often just one fateful click away.

Chapter 3 features interviews with:

- both Moneymakers, Chris and Mike;
- David Gamble, Chris' most appropriately named friend;
- Dan Goldman, marketing director for the online site on which Moneymaker played, PokerStars;
- and Lou Diamond, a one-of-a-kind Vegas character with yet another too-good-to-be-true name. In fact, the name *was* too good to be true. Diamond's real name was Lou Haeick, but he adopted a stage name of sorts for his career as a professional sports handicapper, which led him rather circuitously into a supporting role in the Chris Moneymaker fairytale.

"I didn't know it was a satellite or I never would have played it."

Chris Moneymaker: If I had to take a stab at it, I'd say before I really started playing poker, I was down about $30,000, lifetime, as a gambler. Which, back then, was a huge amount of money for me.

Mike Moneymaker: We weren't really concerned about him starting to play poker, because as far as gambling too big goes, we figured he'd learned his lesson. He once lost like $60,000 of our shared money on sports betting in one weekend. He was a little white and a little green when he told me about it. And he said he was just glad I didn't have a baseball bat in my hand. What he doesn't know is I'd already won it back. I'd made a few bets of my own. Don't tell him that.

Moneymaker: After we started playing no-limit hold 'em in our home game, I started going to the casino down in Tunica, playing there a little bit. Down there, an old guy told me about online poker and I ended up getting on PokerStars and playing.

John Vorhaus: Internet poker dates back to about 1999 or 2000, but it didn't really take off at first. The functionality wasn't quite there and the market wasn't there.

Nolan Dalla: In 2003, that was the first year we had satellite qualifiers to the World Series from online poker sites. Internet poker was still in its infancy, and George Fisher was the first to recognize that we should partner with online poker sites to run satellites, since there were no laws prohibiting it at the time. So George developed a relationship with three or four sites, including PokerStars, and PokerStars agreed to run some qualifying satellites online.

Dan Goldman: The previous year, in 2002, we did a promotion where PokerStars put up two World Series seats and players were able to play in freeroll qualifying tournaments to win these seats. They didn't actually pay for seats, they used Frequent Player Points. 2003 was the first year when we had cash satellites. I think it's the first year that anybody had cash satellites.

Moneymaker: I might have been a losing gambler, but I was a profitable poker player. Back then, the games online were a lot smaller and a lot easier. I almost exclusively played limit hold 'em online, at $5/$10 and $10/$20 if I remember correctly, and I would keep a couple thousand in my account. I started with $200, I believe, and then I would get it up to $2,000, $2,500, and cash out. But leading up to the World Series in April '03, I had 60 bucks in my PokerStars account. I remember I'd cashed out more than I wanted to pay some bills and then I started a pretty terrible poker run. I hadn't had much success in a while playing online.

With 60 bucks in my account, I sat down to play an 18-player sit-and-go, and back then, PokerStars didn't have it broken down all nice and neat like they do now. The satellites and cash tournaments were all grouped together. I saw that there was a $39 sit-and-go with 17 of 18 seats filled and I just clicked on it really fast to try and get the last seat. I just jumped in and started playing. It turned out it was a satellite where the winner earned entry into another satellite where the top three finishers would get a seat in the World Series of Poker Main Event.

To be honest, I didn't know it was a satellite. If I knew, I never would have played it.

David Gamble: I knew he was playing an online tournament. I did not necessarily know the significance—that it was for a seat in the World Series of Poker Main Event. I don't even know that I fully understood what the World Series of Poker Main Event was at that time.

Moneymaker: I won the first satellite. Then I made it down to the final table in the final satellite and I was one of the chip leaders. The top three got seats in the World Series, plus $1,000 spending money. Fourth place paid $8,000 cash. I thought I could maneuver to bust myself in fourth.

The problem was that when five people were left, we started chatting in the chat box, and this other guy with the screen name "Got Milk?" wanted fourth place too. So we were trying to fight over fourth place, and I started losing chips on purpose.

My friend Bruce [Peery] was watching me play from another computer and he saw me starting to lose chips. He called me up and said, "What are you doing?"

I said, "I'm trying to get fourth place. That's the highest cash payout, $8,000."

And he's like, "Dude, don't do that."

I said, "I need money. I get a grand in cash if I win the World Series seat, eight grand if I get fourth. I mean, that's a no-brainer."

He said, "Yeah, it's a no-brainer. Take the dang seat! It's a once-in-a-lifetime opportunity. You'll probably never get to play in that tournament ever again in your life."

But I said, "Why do I want to go play against the best in the world? I play as a hobby. I'm playing for my house."

I figured going out there and playing against the pros, I'm just going to get chewed up. I didn't want to waste my time.

But Bruce convinced me to go after the seat, after promising to give me $5,000 in exchange for half my action. So I went ahead and won the seat.

Mike Moneymaker: He called me and told me he'd won a seat. I said, "A seat to what?"

He said, "The World Series of Poker."

I said, "World Series of Poker? What the hell is that?" I'd never heard of it. I said, "I've heard of the World Series, but that's baseball."

Moneymaker: The week before I left, Bruce told me he didn't have the $5,000 and couldn't do it.

Gamble: Bruce, for whatever reason, backed out, and that created an opportunity.

Mike Moneymaker: Chris told me he wanted to sell a percentage. I said, "Okay, I'll take 20%." People ask if I thought I was making a good investment or just trying to help my kid out. It was a little bit of both.

Gamble: Chris called me. He said, "David, can you meet? I want to talk to you about something."
I said, "Sure. Let's gather."
So we went to a sports bar down in Franklin [Tennessee] and he said, "Listen, here's the deal. I have this seat that I qualified for online, and there was some money put up, but they backed out at the last minute. I got this seat and I've got X amount, but I'm short."
I said, "Well, how much do you need?"
He said the amount and I wrote him a check for $2,000, the same as his dad had put up. It was like buying a lotto ticket.
I wrote him that check, and then I put my credit card down for the hotel room at Binion's.

Moneymaker: My backer was named "Gamble." People ask why that didn't become a bigger part of the story, but I think the story was so surreal, it almost seemed like it was made up already. That detail sort of got lost in the shuffle.

Mike Moneymaker: You know how you get one of those weird feelings? As soon as he called me and told me he'd won the seat, I had this feeling that he's gonna win the darn thing.
I told my wife about it, but I wish I'd written it down and sealed it and put it in a safe-deposit box.

Moneymaker: As a gift of good luck to go out to the World Series, Bruce got me a pair of Oakley sunglasses. He brought them up to my office and gave them to me.

I was real thankful, because I figured I was going to be a tellbox. I really felt like I could go out there, flip my cards face-up and, effectively, play the same way. *These are all pros. They're all going to read me.*

Dalla: The day before the Main Event started, I was walking through the hallway at Binion's and outside the poker office right outside of Benny's Bullpen, there were 37 poker players standing there, all wearing shirts with the PokerStars logo. PokerStars had them signing up for the tournament en masse.

So I walked by and I thought, *Oh, neat. There's thirty-some people coming from this website.* But I didn't think anything of it beyond that.

And I had no idea, of course, but in that line was a certain fella named Chris Moneymaker, who ultimately changed poker history.

Goldman: We had 37 qualifiers entered. The number of players we had accounted for roughly 4.5% of the field. That was the most of any site, by a pretty substantial margin. Nobody was really doing this. PartyPoker, if I remember correctly, in 2003 did exactly what we did in 2002—they bought some seats and sort of raffled them off.

Part of the reason we ran so many satellites was that our players were asking for it and it seemed like a very reasonable thing for us to offer. But the bigger reason was that we knew that it was going to be on ESPN. So we knew that there would be opportunities to get some brand exposure on national television for less than it cost to buy advertising.

Although, looking at it from a business point of view, it

was a little bit controversial—there were a lot of discussions internally over whether it made sense for us to send a measurable chunk of our liquidity to a brick-and-mortar casino. We were pretty small at the time and we're talking about sending $370,000 to Binion's.

Back in 2003, online sites were viewed, for the most part, by casinos and poker rooms as competition. And I'm being kind when I say "competition." I was thrown out of more places than I'd like to talk about. The card rooms in California that we wanted to do business with saw us as a threat, an alternative to playing live poker.

Still, we decided to give this a try, and though some people within the company felt it was a threat to our liquidity, we felt we were in a position where it wasn't going to put us out of business. So we thought it was worth a shot.

Norman Chad: We had a Las Vegas local who Matt [Maranz] hired who helped us a lot with the production, called Lou Diamond.

Lou's one of my favorite people of all time. Lou's such a character. He fits the expression, *If you need anything done, he knows a guy who knows a guy*. Two phone calls and he can get it done for you.

Matt Maranz: I had done an investigative piece on handicappers for HBO's "Real Sports with Bryant Gumbel" years ago and we featured Lou Diamond in the show. These guys, "I've won 50 straight games, pay me and I'll tell you who to bet on"—Lou was a professional handicapper who was selling his picks.

When we had to go back to Vegas for the World Series, I needed somebody who could go get water for the crew and knew where things were, someone who knew the area. So I called Lou and asked him questions, then hired him for a couple dollars a day just to show us where Home Depot was.

He was not a TV guy or anything like that at all. Lou Diamond was a runner for us.

Lou Diamond: Matt gets the job from ESPN and contacts me, and he's just gonna be like a sponge. In the beginning, he just wanted to get some information over drinks and dinner.

We sat for a few hours and talked. And he said, "What do you know about poker?"

So I said, "Uh, more than you. How's that, Matt?"

Deep in the back of my mind, I'm trying to score a job, and I do know more about gambling than Matt will ever know, but I didn't know squat about poker. But I knew I could help him.

So he goes, "Well, here's my dilemma. I need to get the cameras on the winner on Day One—not Day Five when they hit the final table."

I knew how to handicap, and he knows I know how to handicap. So I go, "Matt, you're asking me to pick the winner?"

And jokingly, he goes, "Lou, I'll give you 25 picks and I'll give you three days and you're still not gonna pick the winner."

So I kind of took it as a challenge. "Really, Matt? Okay, just for that, I'm gonna give you the winner."

Technically, I think I was a P.A. [production assistant]. Or I could have been a handicapper. I don't know. There was no official title. But I basically had the worst job and the best job. As long as I had lunch on time and dinner on time and all the snacks when they needed it, I got to play poker all day long as "research."

So anyway, Matt hires me. He says, "Okay, you got a job."

So now I'm working for ESPN—dream, right? I don't care

if I'm the pizza boy, I'm working for ESPN, my check comes from Mickey Mouse. So I'm in the zone. I'm like, *Okay, I gotta find this winner. I gotta do everything I can to impress these guys and lock in a job at ESPN.*

So first thing I gotta do is I gotta get on a satellite and I gotta play a game, so I understand what the hell I'm doing. I get into a $175 buy-in and sure enough, first time I've ever played poker in my life in Las Vegas despite living there 20-some years, and I'm sitting next to Chris Moneymaker. First showdown I ever get in is with Chris Moneymaker.

All of a sudden, he stares at me with them sunglasses.

I got intimidated. I don't get intimidated by anybody. When I tell you intimidated, the goose bumps, hair raising on your arms, everything. Boom. This whole vibe came over me.

So I was like, *Who the hell is this guy and why is he looking at me like this?*

So he beats me. He wins the table.

Afterward, he comes up to me and goes, "Nice game" or whatever. And he goes, "Do you know anybody who wants to buy a seat? I won this thing for $40, I'm broke, I'll sell it for $8,000 right now."

At first I'm like, "Okay, let me see if I can find somebody," thinking maybe I can make a $1,000.

We sit down. We have a drink. We're just bullshitting. And I'm like, "Dude, you gotta play it. You got an opportunity, you know?"

Moneymaker: I don't remember that happening. I know I played satellites beforehand. And I had several beers with several different people. So it's obviously a possibility. But I know I wasn't trying to sell my seat. I wasn't allowed to sell my seat. I was trying to sell pieces of it. I wanted to sell as much as I could, but no one was buying a piece of some random guy that they didn't know anything about who was wearing a PokerStars shirt.

Diamond: I met Moneymaker on a Saturday. Monday rolls around, first day of the tournament, I get into my first meeting with ESPN. All the producers are there. And Matt says, "This is Lou. He's going to try to help us here."

These people don't know who the hell I am. So Matt's first order of business: "Okay, guys, let's get a list of all the people that we want to get the cameras on right away."

They're talking Howard Lederer, Johnny Chan, T.J. Cloutier, just throwing all the big names out there.

I raise my hand. I go, "Guys, I gotta tell you something. I played poker with this guy on Saturday. I get this amazing vibe with this guy, and the kid's name is Moneymaker. It hit me square in the face, guys."

And the laughter afterwards was just like, "Matt, this is the guy?"

Trust me, I was the laughingstock when I said that.

Moneymaker: I don't remember meeting Lou before the tournament, but I do remember him coming up to me on Day Two. I thought he was in some way a member of the press. He was watching the tournament like a press person would.

He came up to me on Day Two and said, "You're my dark horse to win this thing. I like the way you play. You look focused. And I think you're going to win."

And it came true. Pretty sick.

Maranz: Midway through the tournament, Lou said, "I got my pick to win. It's that guy over there, Chris Moneymaker." That's a true story.

Side Action _____

Greg Raymer: When I won the Main Event in 2004, it was my third time playing it. In '02, I bought in for the full $10,000 and I went pretty deep. I finished 80th.

In '03, I won a live satellite from Mohegan Sun to get in and then had one of my shortest Main Event runs when I went broke in the second or third level. I tried to bluff Alan Goehring. That was that.

The year I won, in '04, my story of getting in is a little bit like Chris' story from '03. I would have paid the $10,000 out of my bankroll and played it no matter what, but I actually won the last possible satellite you could enter on PokerStars. It was an 81-player double shootout that cost $160 or so to enter. If you won your first table, you basically got your money back. And then the winner of the second table got the $10,000 entry and $1,000 cash, and a free hotel room if you agreed to wear the PokerStars logo and all that stuff.

I had some backers, so out of the $5 million I won, I kept about $2.9 million.

It's not quite Chris' story of parlaying $40 on PokerStars into the world championship, but history repeated itself to a certain extent.

Chapter 4

Day One

Table 8, Seat 4.

Poker is a game of both skill and luck and in a tournament, the latter speaks first. It is pure random chance that governs at which table you'll start on Day One and who else will be at that table with you—or, to paraphrase Mike McDermott in *Rounders*, whether you'll be surrounded by suckers or whether you'll be the sucker.

It was Monday, May 19, 2003, and everyone in the WSOP Main Event had been dealt one card already. Chris Moneymaker's said Table 8, Seat 4.

When he sat down in that seat at that table, he saw his $10,000 buy-in represented in the form of a stack of chips that added up to 10,000 betting units. You couldn't really call them dollars, because they had no monetary value outside the tournament setting. If you lost half your stack, you couldn't get up and head to the cage and cash out for $5,000. You played until you lost all your chips. Or, for one player in that field of 839 hopefuls spread across 90-plus starting tables at the Horseshoe, you played until you *had* all the chips. Eight million three hundred and ninety-thousand non-monetary-units worth of them.

For 63 players among those 839, there was actual money to be made. The minimum payout, for everyone who finished between 55th and 63rd place, was $15,000. The money gradually escalated from there. If you made the final table of nine, you were guaranteed six figures. Second place would make

$1.3 million. And first place, the player with all 8,390,000 chips, would pocket $2.5 million in actual U.S. dollars.

If you've ever spent time in a crowded casino poker room, you know what Benny's Bullpen sounded like when the tournament began at noon on May 19. The most overdone comparison, but still the most accurate one, is that it sounds like hundreds of crickets chirping. There's some talking, sure, but most players are relatively quiet and serious when the cards get in the air. What you hear instead are their chips, riffling between fingers anxious for something to do.

Poker, of course, involves a whole lot of sitting around, waiting for something to happen, trying to stay centered until cards worth playing are slid your way. So poker players riffle their chips. They do it to announce to the other players, *This isn't my first time at the poker table; see, look at the chip tricks I can do!* And they do it because, well, it beats biting your fingernails.

That 10,000-chip stack you started out riffling could go a long way if you were reasonably conservative. The blinds in the 2003 WSOP Main Event started out at 25/50, meaning the small blind on each hand was forced to pay 25, the big blind was forced to pay 50, and one revolution around the table cost you 75 if you folded every hand. You started with enough chips for 133 times around the table—about 1,200 hands.

Of course, those numbers changed as the tournament wore on. Not only because your chip stack grew or shrunk if you actually played some hands, but also because the blinds went up. After the first two-hour level, they jumped to 50/100. Before long, an ante was introduced. If your stack wasn't growing, it was, in effect, shrinking, because each chip was worth a little less every time the blinds increased.

The more you think about that, the easier it is to understand why so many players riffle their chips. The walls are constantly closing in. If you don't feel at least a little bit of nervous energy when you sit down to play in a major poker tournament, you aren't human.

That's especially true if it's your first major poker tournament, as it was for Chris Moneymaker.

It was also the first major tournament for one other character we'll hear from for the first time in this chapter, Dutch Boyd. The 23-year-old Boyd, probably more than any other voice in this book, represented what poker was poised to become. He was young. He was brash. He was tech savvy. He was a certifiable genius, having started college at age 12. And he was ready to channel all of that genius, not into putting his law-school degree to use, but into conquering the game of no-limit hold 'em.

Chapter 4 also introduces Peter Alson, a noted writer, editor, and amateur poker player from New York who'd been traveling to Vegas to write about the World Series since long before the idea of "poker media" existed in most people's minds.

Of course, that was just one of the many things that would change in the wake of Moneymaker and the 2003 WSOP.

"Wow. Every single player in this room is wearing sunglasses. That's weird."

Norman Chad: When I walked into the Horseshoe, when the thing was beginning, I called up my closest friend back in Washington, the guy who had helped convince me to take the WSOP gig, and I said to him, "Where has this been all our lives?" I said, "I wish you could come out here and look at what I'm looking at, because I cannot believe this backdrop. I cannot believe this group of characters."

My friend is a longtime horseracing writer. He covered the race track for years. And I said, "This makes the race track look like Sunday church! The characters here, the feel of this place, it's unbelievable. I've never been around an event like this."

It was just an incredible first impression. It reminded me of going to Europe for the first time as a teenager with my parents, looking at a whole different culture. This was a great culture that I was so glad to be around. It was gambling, it was gritty—this was the pre-Internet crowd, Amarillo Slim and Doyle Brunson and Howard Lederer and Johnny Chan. It was a great odd cross-section of old-time gambling America.

Barry Greenstein: Each year, the Main Event was getting to be a bigger and bigger thing. It reached 839 players in 2003; the year before was in the 600s. So we're getting 30% growth. That's pretty big growth. In 2003, $2.5 million for first, that was starting to be a lot of money. One of the real milestones was the first time the Main Event hit a million dollars for first place. Now we had a situation where you didn't even have to win it to get a million.

Howard Lederer: Certainly, people were expecting a nice bump in the number of players. But *nobody* was thinking 839. If history was a judge, I think our biggest jump from one year to the next was a little over 100, from '99 to 2000.

Nolan Dalla: We had *just* enough tables to accommodate all the players—Binion's had a warehouse of a pretty good amount of stuff, including extra poker tables. What we didn't have enough of was space. There was a definite lack of space for tables. The sports book was right next to a deli and we had to yank out all the seats there to make room—all the tables and chairs, everything was yanked out of there and we literally threw down poker tables that were of the variety that you'd see in a Thursday night home game, where you had to pull the legs out and pull up some steel chairs. These were horribly uncomfortable metal chairs that the players paid $10,000 to sit in!

But nobody complained. There were lines, there were crowds, there was cigarette smoke, and I didn't hear one complaint about any of it, because it was the biggest World Series ever and people understood that.

Dan Harrington: The tables were spread out upstairs and downstairs, and I was downstairs. I remember the fire marshals being around and there was a big delay in starting, because there was a concern about what happens if there's a fire. Would we be able to get out? I think the answer was, simply, no.

Lederer: It was kind of a checkpoint each year—what's the health of the poker community? What's the growth of the game? How many people are going to play? Everyone was always sweating that number.

You're sitting down at the most important tournament of the year and it really does mean everything to you. No matter how many times you've played in it, you get butter-flies and goose bumps when you walk in there. No matter how experienced you are, you get nervous. You get really excited about it. And that doesn't really happen for any other tournament.

Annie Duke: For me, personally, the '03 World Series was the first time I was asked for an autograph. Someone came up and asked for an autograph and I laughed, because

I didn't actually think they wanted it. I guess people were watching the World Poker Tour on television and starting to become aware of some of the players.

You were definitely feeling the changes in poker. Were you feeling the changes that were to come? Was it 6,000 people descending on Las Vegas? No. But it was the beginnings of what was to come, both in terms of the growing numbers of players and the way that people were considering poker players to be minor celebrities.

Peter Alson: That year was the beginning of feeling like the Internet was having an influence. The number of entrants jumped about 200 people from the year before and we knew that was largely due to the Internet.

Duke: This was the first time you had that huge presence of people who had qualified online and that was almost solely responsible for the jump to 839 players. It seems now like a small number of players that PokerStars sent, but at the time, nobody could believe there were that many of them playing.

Jeff Shulman: The first thing I remember thinking is, *Wow. Every single player in this room is wearing sunglasses. That's weird.*

Greg Raymer: Back then, you tended to know people. You knew most of the names and the faces. If you didn't know someone, they probably weren't very good. Nowadays, I see someone I don't recognize, especially if they're young, I assume they're probably a good online player. He could be the next Internet wizard and I just don't recognize him yet. But that old stereotype, "If I don't know who this guy is, he's probably not any good"—that was a good stereotype. It was usually accurate.

Lederer: You looked across the table and you saw one or two guys with a PokerStars T-shirt on. It was awfully nice of the Internet players to just point themselves out to us.

Harrington: The Internet players were, on the whole, not the strongest players. At that time, the hole cameras were a new institution, so the information had not disseminated to the world yet. No one had time to absorb what good plays were from a strong player. The new wave of books had not come out yet. The teaching tools on the Internet had not yet been introduced. So you had a bunch of people like Moneymaker who won their satellites to get in and they were just cannon fodder. That's how we looked at them.

Chris Moneymaker: My nerves were so bad right before play started on Day One. I was sitting there in the bleachers around the room with my head in my hands. I wrestled in high school and I felt like I was going into a wrestling match—I was nervous, I had butterflies in my stomach. It was bad enough for a guy to come over to me and ask me if it was my first time playing in the event. And then he gave me a crystal for luck.

Dan Goldman: I remember having a conversation with Chris, and this may have actually been the first discussion that we had, in which he was comparing the structure of the World Series to the structure of the tournaments he had played online. That was the point at which I learned that this was his first live tournament.

Moneymaker: Honestly, there was no thought in my head of winning this thing. If I made it through Day One, I'd be happy. If I somehow cashed, I'd be ecstatic. I was in a mind frame of taking baby steps. I couldn't cash until I made it through Day One, so I had to make it through Day One.

The PokerStars guys must have thought I was just a yahoo that had zero chance to win, that I was just burning money. I would go to them and say, "Dude, I got 10,000 in chips, the blinds are 25/50, I don't even have to play a hand! I can fold my way to Day Two!"

Every night, I went to talk to Dan to see who was on my table, and every time I was just like, "I can fold my way to this, I can fold my way to that, I can fold my way into the money!"

That was my strategy for a while: fold my way home. "I can win the tournament. I'll just fold!"

He would say things like, "You don't understand. You can't just keep folding. You're going to have to play hands."

I said, "Yeah, I'm going to play aces and kings and I'll play sets. That's all I'll play."

He said, "You're going to have to open up your range a bit. You can't just sit there. You can't be nervous and play like that."

I'd be like, "Nah, I've got plenty of chips. I'll do what I want to do."

Goldman: I remember getting the sense from him that this structure was so favorable to players that it seemed like he could get his $10,000 back without taking any chances—which was certainly not the goal we wanted him to have.

Moneymaker: I played a pretty snug game throughout the first day. I mean, almost everyone played poker pretty tight in 2003 and I was probably one of the tightest people there. Literally, my whole strategy was to breathe five seconds before I made any decisions. If it was checked to me, I was going to bet. If someone bet in front of me, if I didn't have something I'd fold and if I had something I'd call. If I bet and I got called, I'd only continue if I had something. That was my strategy.

There was no player-specific strategy. I didn't try to steal blinds and antes. I didn't try to accumulate chips without cards. I was the guy that had to have cards to get chips, other than c-betting 100% of the time when I raised pre-flop and they checked to me on the flop. That was the only way I was stealing chips.

And it wasn't because of my nerves. By the time we started playing, or at least after the first 10 minutes, the butterflies moved on and I was pumped and ready to play. I actually felt jacked up and ready to play poker. That quickly waned off, of course, because of how boring poker is.

It was a much more simplistic game back then, and your chips went a much longer way, and I could control my variance. People didn't three-bet very much back then. People didn't four-bet at all, unless they had aces or kings. So I just folded my life away for the first several hours.

I remember having A-K in the small blind in a hand, and a guy raised, and another guy three-bet, and I just folded my A-K. Didn't even play it. I didn't even want to get involved. Stay out of the way.

Lederer: There was a lot of pre-flop limping in 2003. Really, '03 is a year unto itself, in terms of the limping people saw on TV in the Main Event.

The style of no-limit hold 'em, prior to 2003, was certainly not limpy. You had a much tougher field, chock full of pros. A small raise in 1995 or 2001 or whenever was three times the big blind. I was one of the young guns that was *only* raising three times. You'd see the older pros, the Texas pros, raising four or five times the big blind. It was a tight-aggressive style.

What you saw in 2003 was just the beginning of the Internet boom, where all of a sudden you had hundreds and hundreds of these greenhorn Internet players who didn't really know about tight-aggressive. They were just beginners. And beginners limp. So there was probably more limping in that event than in any Main Event before or after. It was just kind of a year unto itself.

By 2004, 2005, a lot of the people winning their seats online had actually logged hundreds of thousands of hands and were real players. Standard raises now are more like 2½ times the blind. Some people just double the big blind. They don't limp, but they bring it in for much smaller raises. That limping thing was mostly unique to 2003.

Moneymaker: When I sat down and scoped out my starting table, I was looking for online patches like what I was wearing. Those were the rookies. Those were the fish. So I talked to them, figured out who they were.

One guy I talked to said he played one-cent/two-cent cash games and won like the 100,000th hand dealt at an online site and then he got a seat, so I was like, *Okay, I want to pick on this guy, because he's probably worse than me.*

As it turned out, there were two noteworthy players at my first table, and one of them was one of these online players, but he definitely wasn't a fish. It was Jim Worth, who was known online as "KrazyKanuck." KrazyKanuck was a name that I actually knew, because he was one of the most successful online MTT players. So immediately, I'm like, *Okay, well, I'll avoid this guy.*

I was sitting in the three- or four-seat, and he was sitting in the eight- or nine-seat. And he raised my blind relentlessly, every single time, for the first two hours. I knew what he was doing—I just had no defense for it. And I didn't really care to have a defense for it, to be honest. I re-raised him one time with kings, and he just folded. But that's the only time I ever gave him any resistance. He knew what I had every time; my hands were playing face-up against him. And he knew how to pick on me.

In between us was the other noteworthy player at the table, Dan Harrington. But Dan Harrington wasn't doing anything. I didn't know who Dan Harrington was. He wasn't wearing one of his bracelets. He just looked like any other older player who was playing the Main Event. I wouldn't have ever thought that he was a Main Event champion.

Dan was sitting over there being as quiet as can be, talking-wise and playing-wise. He was being as snug as I was. He was playing super-tight. So he wasn't even on my radar until a couple hours in, when after he won a pretty decent-sized pot, someone said, "Nice hand, champ."

I had to look at the pictures on the wall of the past champions and see who he was.

Harrington: I absolutely remember playing with Chris that first day, because he was giving me trouble. So I asked around with some of the other pros, "Who is this guy?" And they said, "I don't know. Just some kid off the Internet." That's all they knew. And that's what he was, just some kid off the Internet.

Moneymaker: Late in the first day, I won two real big pots. The first one I had pocket aces against A-Q and the flop came queen-high, so we got it all-in and the guy went broke against me.

Then a little while later, I flopped a set of sevens and got it all-in on the turn against pocket aces.

That was all it took, two big hands toward the end of the day that went my way and I was the big stack at my table.

Dutch Boyd: I got into the Main Event on the very last

satellite that they did at Benny's Bullpen. I wasn't going to be playing it if I didn't satellite in.

I came out to Vegas early, trying to make enough money to buy into the Main Event. I played for about three weeks in Vegas and it just wasn't going anywhere. Kinda stalled out.

So I played a couple of the satellites and it was the very last satellite. They gave away, I think, 11 seats. And I was one of them.

What I remember from the first day of the tournament is something the player to my right said to me. His name was Hua Zhang; everyone just calls him "H.Z." He was one of the better players from San José, where I got my start in poker. At the end of the first day of play, he said something that rang pretty true then and still does.

He said, "You might win this, Dutch, but remember this: If you win, you'll have a thousand new friends, but if you lose, you cry alone." That is so true in poker.

Shulman: Here's a funny story.

My starting table had Mike Matusow and John Spadavecchia and I didn't play a hand for the first hour and a half. I just folded everything. Back then, I pretty much only played pairs and big aces anyway, absolutely nothing else.

All of a sudden, I decided to raise with a 7-5 under the gun and I ended up getting one caller, a kid to my left. I bluffed the flop, then turned a gutshot, and by the river I had the nuts, but the poor kid had the 3-5 for the dummy end of the straight.

I made some little bet and he waited at least two minutes, staring me down, looking like the toughest guy in the world. Then he raised me a couple thousand and he's like, "The action's on you!"

And I was like, *What the hell?* I re-looked at my hand, and I was like, *There's no chance this guy has a 7-5 also.* So I assumed I was up against a set and I did the exact same thing he did. I waited two minutes. I crossed my arms. Then I raised him 2,000, and I was like, "The action's on you!"

Then he moved in on me, so of course I called him and I busted him with my seven-high straight when he had a five-high straight, and I went from like 10,000 chips to 20,000.

And Mike Matusow yelled across the table, "You waited an hour and a half to play the 7-5!"

Greenstein: There were tables both upstairs and downstairs on Day One, and I was downstairs. You started the tournament with 10,000 chips and I remember that as I got to 20, 30, 40, I would hear reports that people were ahead of me upstairs. It's not like now, where you have PokerNews reporting chip counts; those "reports" were all word of mouth. And I specifically got reports that Phil Ivey and Phil Hellmuth had like 70,000 when I had 60,000.

Being a naturally competitive person, I wanted to be the Day One chip leader for no reason other than my competitiveness. So I was playing a lot of hands, and bluffing a lot of pots, and just trying to get ahead of them. And when the day ended, I actually made a bad laydown on the very last hand just to play it safe and be the Day One chip leader, based on hearing that second place was just a few thousand chips behind me. I had A-Q and the board was queen-high, and on the turn, a jack came and I gave it up rather than risk losing a big pot.

As it turned out, the chip-count reports were false and I ended the day with 95,000, while second place only had like 71,000.

But here's what's crazy about my stack size. The table next to mine was Mike Sexton's and he had a pretty tight table. There were nine players at the table and not a single one of them busted on Day One. So their entire table had

90,000 in chips, total, at the end of the day, and I remember Mike saying, "I can't believe it! You have more chips than our entire table."

Side Action _____

Norman Chad: I'd never met Matt Maranz in person before the week of the tournament. So I met him in Binion's in the poker room and one of the first questions I asked him was, "Where's our broadcasting vantage point?"

He gave me an odd look, and said, "Where's our vantage point?"

And I thought since he repeated the words "vantage point," which is a term I never use anyway, I just thought he was making fun of me for using such an erudite term. So I rephrased it, "You know, where do we do it from?"

And he went, "Geez, I've dealt with you for a while. I didn't think you could possibly be as stupid as you look right now. There is no broadcast vantage point. We don't do any of it from here. It's all done in post-production."

I didn't even know what the term "post-production" meant. That we do it all afterward? I had no idea.

Matt Maranz: All the narration and commentary are done after the fact.

One of the funny production flaws from that first year is that, while you're listening to Lon and Norm's narration, sometimes you can see them in the background on camera. They were essentially reporters out there, trying to learn about characters and dig up information for the broadcast. So they had to be out on the floor meeting the players. And there were a couple of times when you'd see them on the broadcast, just past the table. It was a running joke amongst us, like, "Hi, I'm Norman Chad. You might see me right behind there."

Chad: There's an infamous shot from Year One where I'm sitting right there, talking to somebody, while I'm doing the broadcast, plausibly live. There are several of those over the years, but that was the best one, because I'm plainly sitting there watching the thing, while I'm also talking about it on TV.

I wish I could say those are intentional, that those are our Alfred Hitchcock shots to get me into the broadcast.

Chapter 5

Day Two

Other than Lou Diamond, not a single person associated with the ESPN production crew knew or cared about some random amateur from Tennessee, even if his name was Moneymaker, as Day Two of the tournament began. He was just one of 385 players still in the hunt, and plenty of those near the top of the leader board were big-name pros far more worthy of the cameras' attention.

At ESPN's feature table, the only one in the room with hole-card cameras, the focus was on the verbal sparring between Phil Hellmuth, who was nicknamed the "Poker Brat" for a reason, and Sam Grizzle, a colorful veteran with his share of personal history with Hellmuth.

At surrounding tables sat no shortage of stacked pros who seemed much better bets than Moneymaker to go deep. Three in particular among the top six in the chip counts stood out, all of whom knew each other well from the toughest cash-game tables in town.

The chip leader was Barry Greenstein, a mild-mannered former computer programmer who lived in the L.A. area and had been playing World Series events for over a decade, but was just starting to become a serious tournament player.

In third place sat Ihsan "Sam" Farha, whom no one would ever describe as mild-mannered. Originally from Beirut, Farha moved to the U.S. in his teens when the Lebanese Civil War broke out. Though English is not his first language, Farha is one of the great modern table talkers, a slickster (who comes off more like a grifter) with a gift for needling and extracting information with his tongue. In a poker room full of shlubs with untucked shirts, unkempt hair, and unshowered armpits, Sammy stood out with his dapper suits and slicked-back hair. And you couldn't miss his favorite prop/affectation: the unlit cigarette that dangled from his lips from the first deal to the last.

But perhaps the most dangerous player of all was the one in sixth place, with an ominous 66,600 chips. Phil Ivey—whose quotes appear for the first time in this chapter—used a different name when he first started playing poker in the Atlantic City casinos. Back then he was known along the Jersey shore as Jerome Graham, the name on his fake ID. When he turned 21 in 1997, he had to reintroduce himself to the poker room regulars he'd gotten to know over the previous couple of years and explain that his name wasn't Jerome.

Ivey won his first WSOP bracelet in 2000 in a pot-limit Omaha event. Two years later, he *really* forced the poker world to take notice, as he won three bracelets in a single spring, triumphing in a seven-card stud event, a stud hi-lo tourney, and a four-game mixed competition known by the acronym S.H.O.E. That same year, he finished 23rd out of 631 in the Main Event.

When he returned to the Horseshoe in May of '03, he picked up right where he'd left off, making three final tables, including second- and third-place finishes, in the eight days leading up to the Main Event. The 27-year-old Ivey was establishing himself as the best young poker player on the planet—especially when you consider that the highest-buy-in cash games, more so than the tournaments, were really his forte.

Did that make him intimidating for a run-of-the-mill amateur like Moneymaker to have to share a table with? Luckily for Moneymaker, the name "Phil Ivey" didn't mean anything more to him on May 20, 2003, than the name "Jerome Graham" did.

"He was just Phil Ivey—he wasn't Phil Fuckin' Ivey at that point."

Chris Moneymaker: I had 60,000 in chips going into Day Two. I think I was in like 11th place overall. So I was thinking realistically about making the money.

But I overslept and I thought I was going to be eliminated for sure. I figured, *You don't show up, you don't get to play.* It's pretty common knowledge now that your chips just get blinded off until you show up. But back then, I didn't know anything. It was my first tournament. I thought I was done.

And I was like, *What the hell am I going to do? This stinks.* I made it through Day One, I'm going to try to cash, and now I'm thinking that I can't do any of it, because I overslept like an idiot.

Jeff Shulman: Moneymaker was at my table on Day Two, and I remember there was something about his sunglasses where you could see the reflection of his chips and the table. His sunglasses were so shielding of his eyes—that was a little different than what I was used to seeing at the poker table. His were just pure mirrors. So it was sort of like, *I don't know who this kid is, but he looks pretty cool.* I also remember he was drinking a lot of Red Bulls.

Moneymaker: My Day Two table included Johnny Chan and Phil Ivey. I didn't know who Phil Ivey was. He was a young black kid with a lot of chips. I mean, I saw him sit down and I was like, *Oh, that's good. He's got a lot of chips. He doesn't look* *that tough. I'm going to make those* my *chips.* He was just Phil Ivey—he wasn't Phil Fuckin' Ivey at that point.

Phil Hellmuth: I don't think anybody really knew much about Ivey at that point. In '03, he was still young and up-and-coming. I remember he wore a basketball jersey, Houston Rockets, I think. No one really knew who he was back then. Everyone calls him the greatest player in the world now, and I don't know if he is or he isn't—certainly, he's one of the two or three best on the planet—but nobody was calling Phil Ivey the greatest player in the world yet in 2003.

Phil Ivey: I really didn't play that well. I think I was like 27 years old. I played okay, but I was still kind of learning how to play no-limit hold 'em. I had as good a chance to win as anybody, but I was just in there playing on feel.

Moneymaker: I struggled on Day Two, and my struggle was a lot more with Johnny Chan than it was with Phil Ivey. I was sitting in the seven seat, Chan was in like the two seat, and Ivey was two seats to my left, and I think Chan being two seats to *his* left might have slowed him down or something. Ivey didn't really do much that day. But Chan was just abusing me.

Every time I raised, he'd come back over the top. Or he'd put me to a decision. When I was playing with a lot of the pros, I felt like they had aces every hand. Or they flopped sets every hand. I knew in the back of my mind they didn't, but I was playing a little scared.

Some guy told me at dinner one of those nights, "You have monsters-under-the-bed syndrome. You think that your opponent always has the best hand. But they hardly ever do."

After hearing that, it started to sink in that we all get two cards and the pros miss as many boards as I do, so I needed to stop playing fit-or-fold, which is basically what I was doing.

Ivey: Moneymaker made a little impression on me when we played together on Day Two. I remember thinking, *This guy's aggressive.* We didn't play together that long, but he played a lot of pots. He was in there dancing around and I knew he had a shot to win at that point. You're gauging different people in a tournament who have a chance to win, and I honestly thought he was one of them.

Moneymaker: Other than struggling with Chan, I didn't hit any real problems on the second day, other than one big hit I took. I ran A-10 into kings on a 10-high board and lost a big pot. But then we were on a break shortly thereafter.

I came back, flopped a set, and got my stack right back up to where I was. That helped my mental state, and I just kept on cruising.

Howard Lederer: On Day Two, I was at Daniel Negreanu and Phil Ivey's table to start, but I got lucky and that table got broken early.

I moved to a table where I just caught a hellacious rush. I actually bluffed a key pot where if I'd lost, I'd have been down to 5,000, but instead I had like 30,000 at the end of the hand. And then I just went on a rush.

The key hand for me, which took me from like 50,000 to 100,000, Dan Heimiller raised with A-K and I made a medium re-raise with kings, and he called, and the flop came king-high. Not anything special, but it really got me going and I doubled up to 100,000.

Sammy Farha: I didn't play the Main Event a lot, especially before 2003. The payoff wasn't as good like it is these days, so the only way I play it is if there's no other cash game going on. I played it for the first time in 2002. I played so bad, though. I was a chip leader the first day. No one in their life had the chips like I did. But I gambled too much and lost the chips—I don't have a tournament style.

Anyway, in 2003, I was at Binion's and there was no big cash game, nothing going on, so I decided to play the Main Event at pretty much the last minute.

Barry Greenstein: Sammy and I were together at the end of Day Two and I had a straight draw. I semi-bluffed all-in with one card to go against Sammy. He called and I hit my straight on the river. Sammy just got up from the table and started leaving.

I said, "Sammy, you have me covered."

He said, "What's the difference? It's close."

I said, "I think you have 5,000 left."

He said, "Well, what can I do with 5,000? Forget it."

Remember, Sammy's a cash-game player. Sammy's not even a no-limit hold 'em player. He was a PLO player. He was only playing this event because it was the Main Event.

I said, "Come on, you can't just quit."

So he sits down and he goes all-in dark for his last 5,000. Somebody calls him and he doubles up.

The very next hand he goes all-in dark again. Someone calls him and he doubles up to 20,000.

There are seven hands left in the night and he proceeds to play all seven. He did look at the last three or so and didn't get all-in pre-flop. But he played all seven hands.

Farha: I remember I had like 5,400 and I kept going all-in. I had like pocket sevens against A-K, and they stood and

I won the hand. I ended up the day with like 54,000. I went from 5,400 to 54,000 in the span of just a few hands.

Greenstein: I had to almost force him to even sit back down and play, and now he had enough chips to fight on Day Three. Before you knew it, Sammy was one of the chip leaders.

That was funny the way that went down. If I hadn't said anything to him after the big pot we played, he'd have just left the room.

Side Action

Norman Chad: I was sitting around, I think it was Day Two, in the broadcasting tent. I hadn't met most of the 441 people. So I was in the tent and five or six of them were sitting around. They were talking about who they could get to broadcast this thing as a color commentator next year, because they didn't get anybody this year.

I just kind of cocked my head and thought, *Gee, this is a tough business. I mean, I haven't even been on air yet and you're wondering who you're going to get next year, because you couldn't get a real name this year!* I said to myself, *Well, you know, that's the way it goes.*

Chapter 6

The Perfect Name

The question of whether poker can be categorized as a "sport" is a matter of great debate. But if we are to consider it a sport, then "Chris Moneymaker" has to go down as one of the two most appropriate names in sports history, either narrowly ahead of or narrowly behind "Usain Bolt" on the all-time list. (And for third place, feel free to insert your terribly played-out joke about how ironic it is that Lou Gehrig died of Lou Gehrig's Disease.)

Most people, poker fans or otherwise, had never heard of the surname "Moneymaker" prior to 2003. When another amateur named Jamie Gold went on to win the WSOP Main Event in 2006, relatively little was made of his own rather fitting surname, because it wasn't at all unusual; everyone knew a Gold family or two. But "Moneymaker" is uncommon. Chris' ancestors reportedly were in the business of making silver and gold coins and, at some point long before Chris' birth, altered their German last name, "Nurmacher," to "Moneymaker." Simple as that. They literally made money and they adopted a name that spelled it out.

This chapter is loaded with interview subjects reflecting on the name "Moneymaker" and what it meant/means to them. Among those quoted, some of whom haven't been heard from in a few chapters:

- poker pros Daniel "Kid Poker" Negreanu, Howard "the Professor" Lederer, Annie Duke, Barry Greenstein, Dan

Harrington, Kenna James, Jeff Shulman, Cory Zeidman, and Greg Raymer;
- ESPN broadcasters Lon McEachern and Norman Chad;
- ESPN Original Entertainment Senior Coordinating Producer Mike Antinoro;
- 441 Productions Executive Producer Matt Maranz and Coordinating Producer Dave Swartz;
- journalist Peter Alson;
- PokerStars VP of Marketing (and de facto agent for Moneymaker during that week at Binion's) Dan Goldman;
- and Binion's Horseshoe Director of Public Relations Nolan Dalla, who kicks off the action with a classic story of skepticism regarding the name that struck nearly everyone as too good to be true.

"I'm like, 'No, no, what's your real last name?'"

Nolan Dalla: This is something I remember like it was yesterday. At the end of Day One, I've got the chip-count slips, and people all over the world are waiting for this information. We have a bare-bones staff. So it falls on Nolan Dalla to record all the chip counts—after working a 14-hour day, now this workload begins.

There's this huge pile of slips and I've got to sit at my computer and type up the chip counts, one by one. "Doyle Brunson, Las Vegas, Nevada, 23,300." That would be the line. I had to do that for all 385 players who survived the day.

I come across this slip and I was so mad, I couldn't see straight. Because everyone writes their name out, except this guy, apparently. And his name is Chris Moneymaker.

That's what it said, "Chris Moneymaker."

So I'm thinking Chris is his first name and Moneymaker is his nickname. Like Chris "Moneymaker" Smith. Chris "Moneymaker" Jones. I mean, have you ever heard that last name before in your life? I never had.

So my first reaction is, "Who is this joker?" Though I don't think I used the word "joker."

If you go back and look at the official end-of-Day-One chip counts, I think I just put "Chris Unknown" or something. I would not even honor the man by writing "Moneymaker."

The next day comes and I find Chris Moneymaker. This is the first time I'd ever met him. And I say, "Are you Chris?"

He says, "Yeah."

I say, "What's your real last name?"

He says, "Moneymaker."

And I'm like, "No, no, what's your *real* last name?"

Of course, this man has heard this his entire life. He's probably been asked this a million times. So he hands me his driver's license.

I look at it, and all I can do is apologize to him. "I'm sorry. I didn't know that."

Chris Moneymaker: I got asked at least five or six times by WSOP people or ESPN people to show proof of who I was. They didn't believe that was my last name. ESPN didn't want to put that on TV as my name and have it not be true.

Every time I went to a TV table, I had to show my ID to someone else and show that it was not a made-up name or whatever. By Day Three and Four, it was pretty routine that when someone walked up and asked me about my last name, I'd start getting my ID out before they even asked for it.

Matt Maranz: As soon as we heard his name and his story, that he wasn't a pro, that he qualified for $39, that's a no-brainer. You have to follow him. That's a character, just on the name itself.

Dan Goldman: At Binion's, the place where the World Series was played was called Benny's Bullpen, which was on the second floor. You came up an escalator and into this open area, where there was sort of a lobby, and the World Series was played in the next room.

One of the traditions from the World Series that's gone now, because of the magnitude, is that in the lobby area, there was a big whiteboard where they wrote the names of each person who either won or bought a seat. So beginning in February or so when they started to run satellites, you could go in and see three names on the board or 20 names on the board. ·

Then we wired our $370,000 in and there was this huge chunk, right in the middle, of names that were obviously written at the same time.

I remember going up the escalator and coming around the corner and looking at these names, and I knew a couple of the names, so I knew that they had gotten the wire and put our names up. And I saw the name Chris Moneymaker and just for a fraction of a second, I remember thinking, *Yeah, right.* Then I didn't think anything more of it. Because we didn't particularly care at that point if someone was using a pseudonym—which I was 100% certain this was.

Cory Zeidman: I remember seeing Chris Moneymaker's name on this whiteboard where all 839 players were listed. And I thought, *Is this for real? A guy's name is Moneymaker?* I thought it was a fictitious name. I was like, *What kind of name is that?* I mean, had anyone heard of someone named Moneymaker?

Howard Lederer: The first time that I moved to his table, when I heard the name for the first time, it was like, *Really? Is that really his name?*

His name was a bigger deal then than it is now. Now he's just Chris Moneymaker, the guy who won the first big Internet version of the Main Event. Back then, his name created a lot of buzz.

Jeff Shulman: The first time I was at his table, I asked him what his name was, and he said, "Moneymaker," and I thought he was kidding.

I said, "Yeah, I'm a moneymaker too."

Of course, it's a fantastic name. A poker player with the name Moneymaker? It doesn't get any better than that.

Mike Antinoro: I thought it was a joke in the beginning. I thought it was a fake, a made-up poker name. It's too good.

Annie Duke: I heard the name and I was like, "That's a joke, right? That can't be his name." I thought it was made up.

Daniel Negreanu: Like most people, my first reaction was just, "Is that his real name?"

Norman Chad: I thought it was some sort of a stage name, that this guy had adopted this name for marketing or gambling purposes. It was a name that's too perfect to have.

Dave Swartz: It was like, "Well, that can't be real. What's his real name?"

Kenna James: I thought the last name was a joke. And as

it continued to build and we got deeper into the tournament, you were like, "How is this possible, that somebody named Moneymaker is in this position to make all this money?"

Peter Alson: We were saying, "Can you believe that this guy, whose name is Moneymaker, can you imagine what's going to happen if this guy actually wins?" But it also seemed fated somehow—like a guy named Moneymaker is *going to win* the World Series of Poker.

Dan Harrington: It's a classic name.
In fact, I asked the ESPN crew, "If it happens to get heads-up between me and Moneymaker at the end of the tournament, can you announce Moneymaker's name first, so it would be 'Moneymaker-Harrington'?"

Barry Greenstein: Of course, once you get to know Chris, the name evaporates and he's just a nice guy.

Lon McEachern: When I was a TV sportscaster in Southern California in the '80s, we used to run highlights of the World Series every year. One of the reasons I think we started running highlights of the World Series was because Gabe Kaplan made a final table; that made it interesting to the general public. So various media crews were there in 2003 to do their normal fluff piece on this slice of Americana.
One of the crews I ran into was from, I think, CBS Evening News. I think David Dow was the reporter and his producer happened to be somebody I worked with at the CBS affiliate in San Francisco. We hadn't seen each other for several years and I got to catching up with her. I asked why they were there.
She said, "We're here because there's this guy named Chris Moneymaker."

And so the longer Chris Moneymaker stayed, the longer the CBS crew stayed. They were just giddy that this guy named Chris Moneymaker was at or near the top of the chip lead continually.

Goldman: I think it might have been at the end of Day Three or on Day Four, the CBS news affiliate in Los Angeles was in Las Vegas covering the World Series and they wanted to interview Chris. They asked me if I would set it up.

I said, "Sure," and I found Chris and made the arrangements.

The producer said, "Okay, before we put him on the air, I have to ask you a question: Is Chris Moneymaker his real name?"

I said, "You know, I'll be very honest with you—I have no idea. But I'll find out."

So I went and I found Chris, and I said, "Look, I really hate to ask you this ..."

He said, "Yeah, I know." He pulled out his wallet and said, "Yes, Chris Moneymaker is my real name."

As he was showing me his wallet, I heard this voice behind me saying, "Yeah, and my real name is Mike Moneymaker. You want to see *my* ID?"

I turned around, and it was the first time I met Chris' father, who also had his wallet out to show me that his name was Mike Moneymaker.

Side Action _____

Greg Raymer: One of the things that was really cool at Binion's, that you can't do now at the Rio with the numbers they get, was that massive whiteboard hanging on the wall at Benny's Bullpen, where they wrote down the names of everyone who'd entered the Main Event.

One thing I remember about it is that, even weeks in advance, you had names showing up there, because some players had already paid their $10,000. It was great for fueling conversation and gossip. You had some professional grinder, he's like, *It's a month until the Main Event. I've got cash now. I'd better enter now in case I don't have it later.* In other words, you had people who entered early just to save themselves from themselves.

Or you'd see a name listed and think, *Oh, I wonder who put him in! He doesn't have any money!*

Chapter 7

Day Three

At the start of a poker tournament, whether it's the $10,000 WSOP Main Event or a $65 quickie at the local casino, the goal of nearly every amateur entrant is the same: to finish in the money. Any tournament in which a hobbyist turns a profit has to be considered a success for that player.

Most poker pros have grander designs when they take their seats. A minimum cash is hardly worth their time, so some consider anything short of the final table, or perhaps anything short of first place, to be a disappointment.

Then there's the odd exception to all rules, such as a celebrity poker player like Jason Alexander, who recently admitted that his goal in the World Series Main Event is to make Day Four, simply because he's never made Day Four. (These are the luxuries of goal-setting that "Seinfeld" syndication money allows you.)

But for the vast majority of the players in any tournament, the primary aim is to cash. Which makes the stage directly preceding the bursting of the money bubble among the most critically important—and strategically compelling—stages of any tournament.

At the start of Humpday of the '03 Main Event, the Wednesday that represented the third of five days of competition, 111 players were left in the field and 63 would make the money. The tournament organizers' plan was to play down to 45, meaning the money bubble would burst on Day Three.

Chris Moneymaker's starting stack of 100,900 chips put him in 26th place, about 25,000 chips above the average. He probably couldn't fold his way into the money. But if he could just tread water for a few hours, pick up a few small pots here and there, while staying out of harm's way, he'd be able to turn his $39 PokerStars entry into a $15,000 payout. Even after giving half of that to his backers, he'd have a little something to show for his week in Vegas and put a dent in his bills back home.

Players like Moneymaker, amateurs who satellite in and bring above-average stacks to bubble day, are perfect candidates to tighten up like Bruce Jenner's face at this stage of the tournament. You muck that A-J offsuit in early position. You check-fold your flush draw instead of check-raising with it like you did the day before. You try to pick up the occasional small pot, but you don't want to take any major risks and you won't be defending your blinds with rags. All of which makes you the sort of player on whom the pros love to feast for the next few hours, until that 64th-place finisher is eliminated.

Think a $15,000 min-cash matters to Sammy Farha? He doesn't grind it out for three days to make a profit equal to one medium-sized cash-game pot in Bobby's Room at Bellagio. The pros want to go deep or go home. And they pick on all the players who've demonstrably gone ultra-tight, knowing this is their best chance all tournament to run up their stack without needing to show their cards.

It's a fascinating dynamic, and while some amateurs ramp up their aggression and risk going broke, and some pros clam up because they don't quite have enough chips to bully anyone, for the most part, a deep-stacked pro will emerge from those pre-bubble levels significantly deeper than he started.

At the '03 Main Event, no shortage of deep-stacked pros entered Day Three. The chip leader was Amir Vahedi, a wildly aggressive Iranian pro with 303,400 in chips, more than four times the chip average. Vahedi came off as a more affable rough-around-the-edges version of Sam Farha, right down to the unlit cigar he chomped on in place of Sammy's cigarette. He'd won a bracelet in $1,500 no-limit hold 'em earlier in the '03 Series, bringing his confidence to an all-time high. (Vahedi was not interviewed for this oral history, as he died in 2010 due to complications from diabetes.)

In third place sat Scotty Nguyen, the self-styled "Prince of Poker" and the 1998 Main Event champ, with 214,300 in chips. Howard Lederer was about 10,000 chips behind Nguyen in fourth place. For the second day in a row, Phil Ivey entered in sixth place. Not far behind was an amateur who was beginning to turn heads, the telegenic genius Dutch Boyd, who came into the day in 10th place. And in 12th, Phil Hellmuth had plenty of chips with which to push amateurs around, even if his naturally cautious style meant he wasn't likely to do so as ruthlessly as someone like Vahedi.

In short, the vultures were prepared to circle a guy like Moneymaker if he showed weakness or started bleeding chips. He had the stack to make the money. The pressure was on to show that he had the stones to go along with the stack.

Chapter 7 is loaded with insights from the poker players who sat at the tables up to and beyond the money bubble. It also contains analysis and anecdotes from a few off-the-felt names we haven't heard from in a few chapters:

- Matt Savage, the tournament director;
- Brian Koppelman, the co-screenwriter of *Rounders*;
- Bob Chesterman, an ESPN Original Entertainment senior coordinating producer;
- Mike Moneymaker, father of the eventual champion;

- and David Gamble, Chris Moneymaker's friend who, like Mike Moneymaker, had a financial interest in Chris surviving beyond the money bubble.

"Don't worry, kid. That'll never make it on TV—unless you win."

Chris Moneymaker: Going into Day Three, when I looked at the table draw and saw Johnny Chan was two seats to my left, that brought a lot of heartache. Chan was two to my left, and Howard Lederer was on my table as well, and I'd heard he was a really good player and very dangerous. So I was worried about both of them. Dan Goldman told me I was at "the table from hell."

Dan Goldman: It's funny that he remembers it that way. I don't remember using that phrase. But it doesn't shock me at all; he was at a *very* scary table. Not just Chan, but Howard Lederer was there and a couple of other good pros. And this is 2003, when the reputations of Johnny Chan and Howard Lederer loomed even larger than they do today, because they were in a much smaller pool of great players. I remember not wanting to scare him, but wanting him to be alert to what he was dealing with.

We had a conversation about picking up reads on players and the best advice that I could give him was, "You need to be 100% alert. When you're not in a hand, you need to be paying attention and, specifically, you need to be looking to your left and seeing if you have any opportunity to pick up anything on the players acting behind you."

Other than that, there wasn't much I could say. I didn't want to horrify him. But *I* was horrified.

Howard Lederer: Having those stacked tables, that was part of what made the Main Event so amazing. If you're going to win that tournament, sure, it's easier to beat 400 players or 500 players than 8,000 players, but at that time, you were at stacked table after stacked table for five days. You were playing this really slow structure and you were playing all these mind games against people you'd played with for years. In some ways, it was harder, because you were up against such quality players all the time.

So that Day Three table we were at, that was a not-un-usual table—particularly for Day Three, when the field has been thinned considerably.

Moneymaker: It was Table 77. I couldn't find it anywhere. I was looking around for it, and they said, "Well, that's the TV table."

And I was like, *Aw, you gotta be fuckin' kidding me.* I was like, *No, this is not happening.*

Goldman: The table was scary, but at least it was the TV table, so our brand was going to get on TV a bit. And this was at that really delicate tipping point, where we were actually starting to think we might get somebody at the final table. At that stage, having one of our players make an appearance at the final table would be a huge victory.

If you think about it just in monetary terms, we sent $370,000 to the World Series. If we'd been given the opportunity to write a check for $370,000 in return for having one of our players sitting wearing our logo for an entire broadcast on ESPN, we'd have done it in a heartbeat.

Moneymaker: I just told myself, *Don't do anything fucking stupid. Be smart. Don't look like an idiot, please.*

On my first hand that got televised, as millions have seen

on TV, I forgot I had a hand. I was the big blind and I just forgot—I thought I'd folded already.

Howard and Johnny were deep into a hand, Johnny had raised pre-flop, and Howard had three-bet him. I had no information on either of them, so I was trying to pick up any kind of tell I could. I couldn't pick up anything on either one of those two guys and it was really frustrating. So I went into crunch-time study mode, trying to figure out what they might be holding.

I wasn't even paying attention to the fact that it's my big blind, I still have two cards in front of me, and I'm looking like an idiot over here.

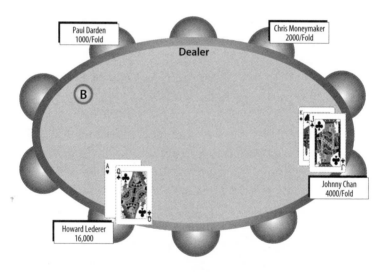

Lederer: I think we were probably waiting for two or three minutes. He just had no idea. I mean, he was an Internet player. In his mind, he'd clicked "fold to any bet." He just got distracted, forgot he hadn't folded—it was kind of weird.

Look, Moneymaker was deliberate. He was not a fast player. So, the first 30 seconds was no big deal. But then it got a little out of hand.

I don't know when I would have said something. It wasn't like I had a super-strong hand. I had A-Q. I don't know that I would've said anything for quite a while.

But Chan only had K-J. He was probably anxious to muck his hand. So he finally said something.

Moneymaker: I remember after I folded, I was red-faced, embarrassed. I couldn't believe I just did that on TV.

But Johnny turned to me and said, "Don't worry, kid. That'll never make it on TV—unless you win."

So I'm like, *Okay, good. I guess that'll never show up on TV then.*

Lederer: Look, it made for great TV. It wasn't that big a deal at the table. It was funny.

Moneymaker: Going through that embarrassment, it actually relaxed me a little bit. At the start of the day, when I found out I was at the TV table, I thought literally if I pick my nose, they're going to show me on ESPN with my finger up my nose. So I'm trying not to scratch my legs, I'm trying not to adjust myself, I'm trying not to pick my nose. I'm doing everything I can not to do anything that you don't want to see yourself doing on TV. So I was just a nervous wreck going into it.

But after that hand, when Johnny told me they're going to edit the coverage, they won't show but a few hands, I was able to relax and be comfortable. I don't have to worry about all the stuff that's going through my head. I can play some hands and I don't have to worry about it being on TV unless I bust Johnny or Howard or something. If *I* bust, no one's going to care. No one's going to want to watch my bust hand.

Kenna James: I was moved to that TV table on Day Three

and I thought it wasn't going to be that big of a deal for me, because all the equipment was behind these black curtains. It was like the Wizard of Oz, you know—*Don't look for the wizard*. The cameras were all kind of out of the way.

But once you got to the TV table, you knew it. It affected me much more than I'd anticipated.

Before that, it was just a grind. I was just playing my game. But when I got in front of the cameras, things changed dramatically. I was getting close to realizing the potential of winning the biggest poker event on the planet, the cameras were in my face, and of course, I was sitting across from Phil Hellmuth, Howard Lederer, Johnny Chan on my left, and the eventual winner Chris Moneymaker settling into the seat to my right.

So the combination of all of that left me with a reality that I wasn't anticipating. I was sitting there, shaking. My body actually started shaking. And I remember us going to break and I went into the parking garage and called my brother back in Michigan, overwhelmed with emotion and really unsure of myself.

What helped me snap out of it was a hand I played against Chris Moneymaker. I had Q-J of spades and I raised. Chris called me from the blind. The flop came down 9-8-5 or something like that. He led into me and I called with a gut-shot and two overs. And then a deuce came on the turn, and he bet, and I thought about it, and I ended up folding. And he showed me Q-J. He showed me the same hand I had. He outplayed me, out of position, with the same hand.

So, after that hand, I said, *I gotta loosen up here. I'm playing too tight and I'm too nervous.*

Lederer: I got into a fun hand with Kenna James that was kind of a precursor to what has happened since, where people essentially hide in their hoodies.

#	Name	Qualifier/Casino
101	TRAPANI, MARKO	BAY 101 CASINO
102	SCHRIER, STAN	SS
103	STORAKERS, JOHAN	POKERSTARS/SS
104	PHAN, YOUNG	
105	WILSON, SAM C.	SS
106	GABRLDAN, FELIX	SANDIA CASINO
107	BRENNAN, WILLIAM	POKERSTARS
108	MANCHON, JOHN	POKERSTARS
109	YAMRON, BRUCE	POKERSTARS
110	KEITNER, ERIC	POKERSTARS
111	PEREZ, EDDY "MR. SOLID"	POKERSTARS
112	KING, JEFFREY	POKERSTARS
113	BEHL, RICHARD	POKERSTARS
114	GOLA, JASON	POKERSTARS
115	FOSSMARK, ANDRE	POKERSTARS
116	PURLE, WILLIAM	POKERSTARS
117	NILSSON, MIKAEL	POKERSTARS
118	THORSON, OLAF	POKERSTARS
119	VAN HORN, BRUCE	POKERSTARS
120	O'CONNOR, PATRICK	POKERSTARS
121	JONAS, TODD	POKERSTARS
122	MAIRHOFER, PETER	POKERSTARS
123	MIZRACHI, ROBERT	POKERSTARS
124	WAN, MANLEE	POKERSTARS
125	MONEYMAKER, CHRIS	POKERSTARS
126	RUSSOMANNO, FRANK	POKERSTARS
127	MANNING, JEFF	POKERSTARS
128	EADIE, JOHN	POKERSTARS
129	CAMPBELL, RAY	POKERSTARS
130	LINDGREN, THOMAS	POKERSTARS
131	WALKER, DANNY	POKERSTARS
132	TAN, VINCENT	DSS
133	CLARK, ESKIMO	DSS
134	SALAMEH, NICOLA	SS
135	KASTLE, CASEY	SS
136	CONRAD, KIRK L.	SS
137	MARSHALL, CARY	SS
138	SHOTEN, CHARLES	SS
139	MAHMOOD, AYAZ	SS
140	WEILAND, BARTON G.	SS
141	SNELSON, GEORGE R.	SS
142	TRAN, AN VAN	DSS
143	FRIEDMAN, PRAHLAD	SS
144	TRAN, ANTHONY	SS
145	HEIMILLER, DANIEL M.	SS
146	HUNTER, KYLE	SS
147	CUMMINGS, MICHAEL V.	SS
148	BARABINO, RICK	SS
149	WILSON, MARTY	SS
150	McDONALD, IAN	SS

151	LILES, M
152	ADAMS,
153	BRAYER,
154	EDWARDS
155	FAGAN
156	KOZIC
157	TEIXEIR
158	BOWEN
159	KROG
160	AL SPAC
161	CHAKRA
162	ATKIN
163	BARATO
164	PLONA
165	DOBO
166	HUTS
167	BUCKF
168	ENGEL
169	KAPOU
170	RIDER
171	JACO
172	EVANS
173	LAAK
174	SHER
175	BERG
176	TSCH
177	AKIY
178	JOHN
179	DUN
180	KIS
181	FAN
182	LIN
183	RE
184	BL
185	CH
186	CA
187	PF
188	BV
189	SE
190	A
191	S
192	Z
193	
194	F
195	
196	
197	
198	
199	
200	

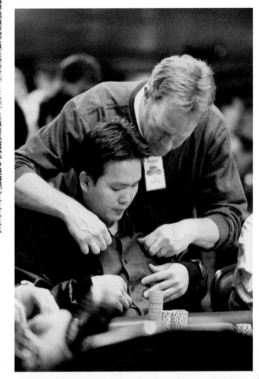

LEFT: In 2003, one name found among a list of PokerStars qualifiers on the famous Horseshoe whiteboard made everyone do a double take: "Chris Moneymaker."

RIGHT: A member of the ESPN production crew mics up a player at the featured table.

BELOW: Moneymaker (far left) at the "table from hell" on Day Three, with Kenna James (hand on chin), Johnny Chan (black T-shirt), and Paul Darden (foreground, shaved head).

LEFT: 441 Productions' Dave Swartz and Matt Maranz, co-inventors of the modern-day televised poker tournament

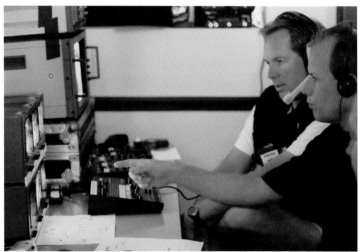

ABOVE: Behind the curtain, 441 employees watch video feeds from the hole-card cameras.

LEFT: Binion's Horseshoe Media Director Nolan Dalla, possibly the most overworked man in Las Vegas in May '03

ABOVE: With the last 10 players seated at the unofficial final table, Moneymaker (back to camera, in PokerStars jacket) gets involved in a critical hand with Phil Ivey (across from Moneymaker in basketball jersey).

BELOW: After Ivey busts, the official final table poses for photos. From left: Dan Harrington, David Grey, Chris Moneymaker, David Singer, Jason Lester, Young Pak, Sammy Farha, Tomer Benvenisti, and Amir Vahedi

ABOVE: Three players remain at the final-table soundstage; Tournament Director Matt Savage calls the action leading up to former champion Dan Harrington's elimination.

BELOW: The gravity of heads-up becomes real for Moneymaker as two shotgun-wielding guards and a box containing $2.5 million in cash make their way into Benny's Bullpen.

ABOVE: Farha and Moneymaker strap on their poker faces as they prepare to bully and bluff heads-up, the title of World Champion of Poker at stake.

BELOW: Liars, guns, and money. The pedigreed pro represented everything poker had long been; the amateur online dreamer represented everything poker would become.

LEFT: Farha and Moneymaker discuss a deal, but Sammy shows his hand and Chris knows how to play him.

BELOW: Moneymaker's aggression belies his nervousness.

LEFT: Moneymaker celebrates by raising two bricks—more money than he'd ever made in a year.

RIGHT: An ESPN hat that Chris signed for Lou Diamond, the handicapper who believed in Moneymaker from Day One

RIGHT: Mike and Chris Moneymaker enjoy a champagne toast.

BELOW from left: Dan Goldman, Becky Behnen, Benny Behnen, David Gamble, Mike Moneymaker, Jim Miller (co-tournament director), Bruce Peery

BOTTOM LEFT: PokerStars Vice President of Marketing Dan Goldman

BELOW: The new champ poses at the scene of the Cinderella story.

Phil Ivey

Greg Raymer

Phil Hellmuth

Erik Seidel

Howard Lederer

Dutch Boyd

Daniel Negreanu

Barry Greenstein

James: There was a lead-up to that hand that nobody knows. The conversation at the table was centered around sunglasses and people using them to protect their eyes and their face. People were on both sides of the fence on that, thinking different things about whether sunglasses should even be allowed. I was kind of quiet as far as my position on it.

Then I suddenly got this funny thought. *What would it be like if somebody was sitting here playing, headless?* You know, like a headless horseman! I'm thinking about this image of my jacket with just the baseball cap on top of it, so it looked like a guy with no head. That was what I was thinking about before this hand came up against Howard Lederer, where I had pocket queens.

Lederer: He made a big bet. I believe he had it, right? I don't remember the hand exactly. Certainly, I had a reputation as being a pretty good reader of people. And he knew I had to take a read.

James: He raised with pocket sixes, I re-raised with queens, and then I zipped my jacket up over my head. It really wasn't out of fear. I know people took it as me being scared or intimidated by Howard's stare, but it was more like, *I'm going to loosen up and have fun.*

I mean, I had two queens. I wasn't that afraid that I didn't have the best hand. It was a combination of me wanting to loosen up and get out of this nervous mode that I was in, along with tying in what everybody was saying about sunglasses in poker. So I just went with it and said, "Hey, take a look at this." I'm covered up, giving him nothing to look at.

Then I unzipped my jacket a little bit and took a peek out. I was having a lot of fun.

Then Howard said, "You can come out now."

Lederer: I laid down. It's hard for a guy who's bluffing to be goofing like that and that's the decision I made. So I think hiding in the jacket didn't really help him. But it was just a fun hand.

Moneymaker: I had one hand against Howard, the first time I moved all-in all tournament. I had aces and he had A-K, the flop was three little cards, and I went all-in. He folded and I let out this big exhale, but the big exhale was a little bit of an act. I wanted Howard to think that I was weaker than I was. I was relieved he folded, but honestly, I wasn't that nervous.

Back then, if I had aces, they might as well be quads. And if my memory is right, I'm almost positive this hand was after the money bubble had burst.

Lederer: One of the most memorable hands of the day for me was a laydown I made against Johnny Chan. He moved all-in on a 3-7-7 flop and got me to fold pocket eights.

That was a tough hand and I wrote a blog about it. In the blog, because the tournament hadn't aired on TV yet, I didn't know what he had [A-3]. Basically, I put him on A-K or a big pair. And I just felt like given that range of hands—and Johnny's a tight player; he really peddled the nuts more than people might think—I just wasn't ready to put that many chips at risk in a spot where I thought the best-case scenario was that I was still going to lose 20% of the time to two overcards.

I don't regret the fold that much. I felt like I might have the best hand, but you know, you're never going to win a tournament if you never fold the best hand. You're just not folding enough. So I don't have any regret—even though now, knowing the cards, I should have called.

Brian Koppelman: Johnny Chan was poker's Joe Frazier or Muhammad Ali. That guy won two years in a row, back to back. And sure, our movie made non-poker people know who he was, but Johnny was the most famous poker player already. We wanted Johnny in the movie, because we thought Johnny was the bad-ass cold motherfucker.

Matt Maranz: Johnny Chan is this great poker player who even my wife knew about because of *Rounders*.

Koppelman: If you wanted to say that Moneymaker's run tapped into the home poker player's fantasy, certainly the home player who watched *Rounders* a bunch of times and now sees some accountant knock Johnny Chan out of the tournament is getting to live vicariously through this guy.

Moneymaker: It was the last hand before a break, not the last hand of the day—they might have edited it a little bit there to look like the last hand of the day.

Lederer: I wasn't at the table. I left for that hand to go on break and I didn't witness it. I came back from the break and Chan was gone.

Moneymaker: It was an ace-high flop with two hearts and I had A-8 of hearts. I bet, he raised, I put him all-in, and Johnny called. He had K-5 of hearts.

I was 100% shocked that he made that call with that hand, because I was still suffering from monsters-under-the-bed syndrome, thinking that the pros always have monster hands. When he called, I thought I needed to catch a heart. I thought I was behind; I thought he had A-K or better.

Obviously, I had the nut flush draw and I really liked my hand, but when he did call so quickly, I was like, *It's Johnny Chan. There's no way I'm ahead. I gotta get lucky.*

When he flipped his hand up, I was more than shocked to see him put his money in that bad. Knowing what I know now, it's not really that bad—he had to catch a super cooler for me to have the hand I had. He flopped the second nut flush draw with a gutshot. He check-raised me, he had a lot committed to the hand, it's not like he called off 100 big blinds or something. I don't think he would do anything different today, to be honest. He knows he's behind, obviously, but he was committed and he figured he had at least nine outs. He just ran into the one hand he didn't want to see.

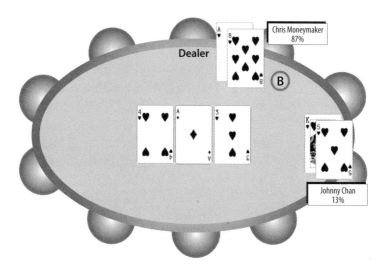

Matt Savage: As a member of the staff, you're thinking, *Boy, this would be really great if Johnny Chan could get to the final table, and win the tournament, make history by winning his third Main Event bracelet.*

Moneymaker was a nobody—this kid that won his way

in online—so we didn't know how that would be perceived, and him knocking out these players that are supposed to be world champions, it could change the way poker is viewed. I mean, if an amateur wins, is that bad for poker because it suggests that the game is all luck?

We were all curious how it was going to be portrayed on TV. I remember thinking, *It's not good for the World Series that Chan is out.*

But as it turns out, it was the best thing that could have happened.

Nolan Dalla: We wanted to have this all-star lineup at the final table. This was our ESPN debut broadcast, so we wanted—and ESPN wanted—to have a Johnny Chan or a Doyle or a Hellmuth. So when Johnny Chan was eliminated, there was certainly some disappointment in that.

Maranz: Our coverage, we started with like 40 players we were tracking from the very beginning. It didn't dawn on us that none of these players would be around at the end. But then as guys got knocked out, we'd pick up other players to follow.

At that point, of course, you have no idea who Moneymaker is, and Johnny Chan is Johnny Chan. So you start going to Plan B.

Lon McEachern: You go find a hero that people want to see and if he gets knocked out, then the person that knocks him out, he becomes the hero and you can follow him. It's a brilliant progression that Matt made. Every step was just perfectly placed like a jigsaw puzzle to the end.

Moneymaker: That was the hand that won me the tournament, because of the confidence factor. I'm like, *Okay,*

I'm in the money. I just knocked out Johnny Chan. This is gravy from here. I'm not playing too bad, I'm making good decisions, I've never been all-in, I haven't been at risk. I'd increased chips every single two-hour level except for once on Day Two. So my confidence was getting higher the whole time. And that makes the game pretty easy.

Chan was literally one of three poker players I knew of before I left for Vegas, and I believed he was the best poker player alive. So for me to knock him out and have him crushed the way I did, my confidence level went through the roof and my game opened up and I started playing with more freedom, realizing that if the best player puts his money in that bad, maybe the skill gap isn't that big. When I busted Chan, that was like beating Mike Tyson.

David Gamble: I had a business trip that conflicted with the start of the tournament. When I got there on Wednesday, he had just knocked out Johnny Chan.

It was Chris, Bruce [Peery, Chris' close friend], and I. We stayed together in the same room the rest of the week. The room didn't have air conditioning! It was a double room that was hot as all get-out. It was a dump. Then, as Chris was winning, they were going to upgrade us, but he was superstitious: "We're not changing anything."

They both snore like bears, and so do I, and I was like, "Oh, Lord."

He didn't want anybody coming in the room, didn't want them making the beds. We took the same path to the poker room every day. We wore the same shirts and hats.

Mike Moneymaker: I went out there with Chris for the weekend leading up to the tournament, then I came home on Monday, Day One. He'd been playing a couple hours when I left. I said, "Hang in there, boy. If you do good, I'll be back."

Bruce called me right after he knocked Johnny Chan out. And about a half-hour later, Chris called and said, "I knocked Chan out. Can you get back?"

I said, "I already booked a flight."

Dutch Boyd: Day Three was when I started really building up a good chip stack—I think I ended Day Three second or third in chips. And I remember, maybe about halfway through the day, one of the coolest things that happened to me, probably still in my poker career, was [1972 world champion] Amarillo Slim [Preston] came up to me and he said that he was picking out like 11 horses against the field, and he was thinking about putting me on his list. And he was wondering if I played poker at all, how I got where I was.

I told him that I wasn't new to the game, I was a prop [a player paid by the house to keep the games active] from up in Garden City.

So he picked me as one of his horses to win the whole thing against the field. That was really cool.

Sammy Farha: The first time they showed me on TV, they described me as an investor from Houston. I was a full-time poker player. I was never an investor. But I gave that image to a lot of players. I built that image and poker was different back then. Today, everybody knows who you are. In '03, it wasn't like this.

So I pretend like I'm an investor from out of town, just to get the game going. I was a full-time pro. But back then, before poker was on TV, they didn't know who I was, they want to play against me. And I'm breaking them one by one.

Daniel Negreanu: I played with Sammy on Day Three and it was clear that he had control of the table. He had a big stack of chips and he was talking his way through a lot of hands and he was really confusing a lot of people. When I sat at the table, he was the guy I was worried most about.

Phil Hellmuth: I remember Scotty Nguyen was telling stories about how he bluffed Sammy Farha—how Sammy had folded top pair and a flush draw and Scotty had nothing. I remember Scotty bragging about that. And I remember thinking Scotty's insane, because you can't bluff Sammy Farha.

Jeff Shulman: Sammy was such a thrill.
I played with Sammy a lot before then and I just couldn't figure him out. I was pretty good at putting people on hands, but I could never put him on a hand. He was like Gus Hansen and Phil Ivey before they emerged. He would just put pressure on and boy, the way he was able to get to like 200,000 in chips before the next guy even had 30,000 or 40,000, it just happened over and over. And then he would lose them somehow.

Farha: I *am* a crazy player, but within reason. It's marketing. I'm marketing myself as crazy. Which, I am crazy, but I know when to lay it down, at least.
I remember, one hand, I laid down top two pair. And if I called, I would have lost. The guy showed me bottom set.

James: When I think of Sammy Farha, I think of somebody who's very creative. And I think of the unlit cigarette. Sammy doesn't smoke, by the way. But he's very superstitious.

Negreanu: I had a hand against Sammy that, for me, was a learning lesson. I opened the door for him to outplay me in a situation where today, I would have been more cautious.

It's pretty much the only hand I remember from that World Series.

It went check-check to the river, and the river came the nine of hearts, which made me three nines, but it also made a flush possible. He bet, and I got aggressive and raised with the three nines, and then he re-raised me all-in.

When I folded, he showed me the ace of hearts. So he either had the ace of hearts with another heart, or just the ace of hearts alone, knowing that I couldn't call him because I didn't have the nut flush. He either had the nuts or he was just pretending to have the nuts.

That hand was a real epiphany for me about being more respectful against certain players. I felt Sammy was trying to push me around, but I didn't know for sure. I should have called his bet instead of raising. I hadn't really considered what happens if he re-raises.

Hellmuth: I had a pot against Sammy that really hurt me. That was a huge pot in that tournament. Sammy Farha had never done well in a no-limit hold 'em tournament, ever, that I'm aware of. He was considered a great pot-limit Omaha player, but I don't think that anybody gave him a chance in this tournament. And I got into this hand with him that really set me off.

Farha: At that time, I wasn't good friends with Phil Hellmuth. We never played together; he's a tournament player, I never played tournaments. And I know he's going to pay me off. I know Phil talks a lot, but he pays off a lot. And I gambled with the hand. Nothing wrong with gambling with a hand.

He said, "Sammy Farha will never make it to the end. Nobody plays that hand."

Hellmuth: He called a big re-raise pre-flop with Q-J suited and I had K-Q offsuit. They didn't have hole-card cameras on that table and I may have told the production guys later that I had A-K, but I had K-Q. I remember the hand well, trust me. And he called the re-raise.

It came K-9-3, two diamonds. He checked, and I checked behind him, because if he had a set or a straight or a flush draw and was going to push on me, I didn't want to be taken out of the hand. Also, it set up a trap where he'd be forced to bet or he might take a bluff at it. So for a lot of reasons, I checked.

Then he turned a flush. He bet and I called, and on the river, he bet, I called. And that was one that kind of set me off a little bit, because hold 'em players, in those days especially, you didn't call a re-raise with a Q-J suited. It was considered a very poor play. So that set me off into my usual tirade.

Farha: I had a lot of chips and his re-raise wasn't that big. And sometimes you gotta gamble if you know your opponent's going to pay you off. If it's somebody else besides Phil, I wouldn't gamble with them. But he didn't raise me a lot, so I played the hand and I caught a monster flop.

And he played it *so* well. He checked on the flop, then when I made the hand, he just paid me off. All the way.

I still like Phil, though. I just don't like the way he handles strangers, calling people donkeys. That I don't like. But I like him personally.

Hellmuth: When you've played for three or four days to get somewhere, to make it down deep, and then someone does something that is horrendously bad and it ends up costing you, it's tough. I used to just see the injustice in it and go, *Wow, I played great for 18 hours, someone lost their mind, played a hand as bad as they could play, forced me into being a* *champion and making the right move, and then I get screwed by the deck? Really?*

Cory Zeidman: Everyone who's played with Sammy has a Sammy story, right?

Mine is, we were down to 46 people; this was the end of Day Three. We had a break and then we were going to play down to 45. So on the break, ESPN did an interview with me. And at this point, I was getting pretty short on chips.

They interviewed me and asked about surviving the rest of the day, and I'm like, "Look, I'm not just looking to survive. I'm still planning on winning this thing," and so on and so forth. And then the interview ended and I went back to the table.

At my table, one of the big chip stacks is Sammy. And right after the interview, I get dealt pocket jacks. Sammy had made a raise and I went over the top all-in.

Sammy's contemplating what to do. And the cameras are filming this. He's contemplating, so I'm afraid he might have A-Q or something—and to be quite frank, at this point, I'm looking for him to fold any hand. Even if I have an edge, I want to survive the day, because I have that interview in the back of my mind.

I had no idea it wasn't going to air, of course.

I'd just done all this trash talking and I'm like, "Look, Sammy, if you call and beat me, I might look really bad, because I just had this interview with ESPN and I went into this speech that my friends and family are going to see, how I'm going to not only survive this day, I'm going to win this thing, and if you knock me out now, I'm going to look really bad to my friends and family." So I'm going on for at least five minutes like this.

Eventually, Sammy folded and said, "If you go on to win this thing, you owe me a steak dinner."

Bob Chesterman: It was somewhere around this point in the tournament that the Binion's people approached me, asking me to extend the tournament. All these people were showing up and they were realizing that this was good for business, so they wanted to add extra events at the end and have us keep the cameras out there.

But obviously, you go out to an event like this, you have everybody on the production team booked for a certain amount of days, then everybody's off to their next thing. That was a funny thing. I remember having to explain to them that we couldn't extend things any further or stay any longer.

Side Action

Chris Moneymaker: I knew there were going to be some questionable edits, because after the tournament was over, the guys from 441 Productions called me up and asked me what my hand was on one specific occasion, because they didn't catch it on camera.

So I knew right then, if they're calling to ask me what my hand was, they're just guessing at some stuff.

Matt Maranz: A lot of times people blocked their hole cards. Not intentionally. Guys playing 200, 300 hands a day, the thumb goes over the cards sometimes, or the chips accidentally block the view. It's not something that happens very often, but what we would do a lot of times is we would call players to verify.

What we learned is that players lie about their cards. After the fact, why would someone lie? But they do.

Over the years, having to verify the cards happened less and less. And for the fans, sometimes it was fun for the viewers not to know. We would play the hand blind.

Kenna James: I had a pivotal hand with Howard Lederer where we didn't get to see his cards. I had pocket eights and I think Johnny Chan had something like pocket fives with the five of clubs, and the flop came down 2-3-4, all clubs, so Johnny flopped an open-ended straight-flush draw. I had an overpair with the eight of clubs. And here's Howard betting into us.

Johnny and I both folded. I folded the overpair with the eight of clubs, and Johnny folded an open-ended straight-flush draw.

I guess we both felt that because Howard was out of position and he was leading into us, we felt like he must have had it.

Howard Lederer: I had the nuts. I flopped the ace-high flush. I think I had like A-Q, I'm not exactly sure, but I know I had the ace-high flush.

James: Wow. Wow. That is good to know after all these years. I honestly never knew. For me, that was a pretty big lay-down at the time. And then when I saw Johnny's laydown on TV, to fold the open-ended straight-flush draw, wow.

Chapter 8

Day Four

Whenever a politician tries to either ban or legalize poker in some shape or form, we're inevitably fed the "luck vs. skill" argument.

Is poker a game of luck? If so, then it must be a form of gambling and it should be treated as such.

Is poker a game of skill? If so, then it should be viewed no differently than chess or golf or any other game that every human has the freedom to play.

Anyone who has spent a significant amount of time playing poker knows that the whole luck-skill argument is misguided. There's really nothing to argue about. Poker is a game of skill. It's also a game of luck. End of discussion.

In the short term, luck can determine the outcome.

The longer you play, the more the law of averages takes over, luck evens out, and skill determines who wins.

Anyone who denies the presence and importance of either skill or luck in poker is either willfully and monumentally ignorant or mentally unfit to be making decisions for themselves or anyone else.

In any single poker tournament, luck plays a *huge* role. However, the slower the structure of the tournament, the smaller that role. So in a five-day tournament such as the WSOP Main Event, with two-hour levels and a starting stack 200 big blinds deep, the luck factor is relatively manageable. But you do need to get *somewhat* lucky to win in a field of hundreds of players. At the very least, you need to avoid getting unlucky in key spots.

Poker is a unique game in that bad play can be rewarded, while perfect play can be punished. With that in mind, it's fair to suggest that if Chris Moneymaker had been a better, more experienced poker player than he was in spring 2003, he almost certainly wouldn't have won the world championship.

On Day Four in particular, luck stepped up to assist Moneymaker. He came into the day sixth out of 45 remaining players, with a stack of 357,000 in chips, so he could afford a misstep or two even if luck *didn't* bail him out. But it did— once when he made a mistake and put himself in a position to give away many of his chips, once when he was on the wrong end of a cooler until a river card put him on the right end, and once when he made a daring, correct, but risky call that most pros wouldn't make and proceeded to dodge the potential bad luck of a knockout punch.

Luck is a key component of poker, because it brings the fish into the game and, often, keeps them swimming for a little while. You can't luckbox your way into suiting up for the Miami Heat or throwing pitches in the ninth inning of Game Seven of that *other* World Series. But in poker, the presence of luck gives anyone a chance.

That said, you'll never make it to the final 45 of the WSOP Main Event without some skill, and the leaderboard entering Day Four was *stacked*.

The chip leader was French poker legend Bruno Fitoussi, loaded with ammo at 671,500 in chips. Dutch Boyd was in a distant second place, 180,000 chips behind Fitoussi. The next two spots were held by former world champions, Scotty Nguyen and Phil Hellmuth. Sam Farha sat in seventh place. The top 20 also included the likes of Amir Vahedi, Howard Lederer, former champ Dan Harrington, Freddy Deeb, Minh Nguyen, Jason Lester, Jeff Shulman, and Marcel Luske.

And in 16th place coming into the day, with 227,000 in chips, stood a player who makes his first appearance in the oral history in Chapter 8. Humberto Brenes hailed from Costa Rica and had been playing at the WSOP since 1987. He placed 14th in the Main Event in his first try, and the very next year, he went all the way to final table, finishing fourth. In 1993, he won two bracelets. Brenes was a highly respected player, a colorful character, and, as it turned out, a man destined for an important role in Moneymaker's remarkable run.

"The guy had big balls. And that's a very important trait."

Howard Lederer: We're getting ready for Day Four and I see Humberto Brenes in the bathroom right before we're about to play. Humberto is flashy and loud at the table, but he's a really tight player.

I wished him luck, and the way I did was I said, "Well, I sure hope that the best hand holds up for you today, Humberto." I knew that if he got all his money in, he'd probably have the best hand.

A few hours later, I heard that he got busted by Moneymaker, where of course he got all-in with the best hand and Moneymaker hit the two-outer. He had aces against Moneymaker's eights, and the flop was like K-9-2, and Moneymaker put him all-in with eights and spiked his eight.

Chris Moneymaker: I can't remember what hand I put Humberto Brenes on, but I didn't put him aces, of course.

Pre-flop, I think I raised and he re-raised on the button, and I flatted. The flop came king-rag-rag, which I figured didn't connect with a lot of his hands. The hands he could have here that beat me were aces, kings, or A-K, and for some reason I didn't put him on any one of those hands.

I ended up check-raising him all-in on the flop, because he did something that he did when I played with him the day before, when he was completely bluffing against David Grey: He got up and sort of did a little move. He did the same thing the day before and he showed a bluff, so I made my mind up.

I felt like I had pretty good instincts, pretty good reads. And my read was that he was beat, so I went with it. Obviously it was incorrect, so I had to go to Plan B and suck out.

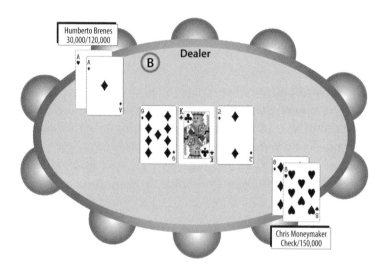

Dan Goldman: The Humberto Brenes hand, if you watch it on TV, you'll see this guy in a black jacket standing behind Chris. That's me. When the eight comes off, Chris jumps up and grabs me and dances me around. And he actually turns me with my back to the camera, which shows the PokerStars logo.

When that broadcast first aired, our traffic spiked by a factor of 10.

Chris' logo was on his hat; You could barely see it. But my logo was like a foot tall on the back of my jacket. In fact, probably four or five months later, I was at an airport somewhere and I was wearing the same jacket and somebody came up to me and said, "Were you in the World Series of Poker?"

And I said, "No, I'm involved with a company that's involved with the World Series of Poker."

He said, "You were there for that hand with Chris Moneymaker and Humberto Brenes!"

And I thought, *Wow, my 15 minutes of fame came from hugging the guy who was getting his 15 minutes of fame.*

Humberto Brenes: I lost with two aces versus Moneymaker with two eights. But I have no bad feelings about losing this hand. It was good for the whole poker world.

Moneymaker gave us an explosion. He pushed the button for the explosion in poker and all of poker won.

I lost the hand, but I feel like a winner after being part of such a great moment in poker history.

Goldman: After that hand, I called my bosses at PokerStars and said, "This guy's actually got a shot."

Obviously, I can't say that's a genius play he made. But what it told me was that he was beyond the point where he was afraid to take big risks. And he wasn't going to make the final table if he didn't play aggressively and if he didn't get this idea out of his head that he just needed to climb up the money chain.

That hand told me that the guy had big balls. And that's a very important trait.

Lederer: Look, he got lucky. He moved in with eights against Humberto and hit his two-outer.

But that also scares the shit out of you when you hear

about that hand, because he's capable of anything.

It wasn't like I had a lot of respect for him or his game. But I had respect for what he was doing. He was mentally tough.

Dan Harrington once told me that one of the most important things you do in a poker tournament is you try and identify the guy at the table at that moment who wants to leave. For some people, that's right at the beginning of the tournament. Just the pressure of being in the Main Event is making them so uncomfortable that they want to get out of there.

When you get into Day Two, then Day Three, now you're approaching the money. The pressure gets ramped up and people respond to it differently.

Whatever stage you're at in the tournament, usually there's someone at the table who's at the point where if he makes a bad play and goes broke, it's not so bad, because he's out of the pressure cooker.

I was always waiting for that to happen to Moneymaker, and it never did.

He wasn't the greatest player, but he was tough as nails and he was unpredictable. And it was always in the back of your mind, *Well, I have no idea what this guy has.* And he used that to his advantage. He had some deficiency on the skill side. But he was hard to deal with. He put pressure on people. You could feel him at the table. You weren't happy he was there—you would much prefer some other Internet player freaking out and giving away his chips. So I have all the respect in the world for what he pulled off, because it's just not easy to keep your cool.

However, I should say that a player like Moneymaker has one big advantage over a player like me: He doesn't feel the enormity of it. He hasn't spent his whole adult life trying to win this thing.

The very first time I played the Main Event, I finished fifth. And it didn't hit me. It was a big deal to be playing in it, but it wasn't my whole life. I was a cash-game player from New York.

But by 2003, the Main Event was a huge deal to someone like me. That kind of pressure builds and it doesn't help. But Moneymaker's not feeling those things.

Kenna James: Pressure is subjective. The more pressure you feel you're putting on yourself, the tougher it becomes. I put so much pressure on myself that I let the situation overwhelm me. I finished in 38th place. When I busted, it was almost, sadly to say, a relief.

Cory Zeidman: I got knocked out on a three-way all-in—Kenna James got knocked out on the same hand. This guy had pocket jacks, and he thought about it forever to call us. I had pocket fives, I moved all-in, Kenna called with like A-Q, and this guy thought forever. When he finally called and showed his hand, we were stunned, like, *How did it take you so long?*

If he would have folded, I would have beaten Kenna and survived. But because Kenna had more chips than me going into that hand, he was given 38th place and I was given 39th.

Moneymaker: The most important hand I played that you didn't see on TV was against a guy named Chuc Hoang. I can't remember the blinds exactly, but he raised and I called. Then we went check-check on the flop. The turn came around and I had A-3, which was complete air. He made a tiny bet, 15,000. So I decided I was going to raise 15,000. And then he came back over the top of me another 15,000.

At this point, I'm thinking, *Okay, he's got a decently strong hand,* but I'm a stubborn son of a bitch and I think I can get him off of it, so I make it 100,000 more. And he calls.

At this point, I'm like, *Oh, this is not really the spot I want to be in.* I've got no outs at this point, I assume. I've just gotta hope for a good card on the river that doesn't change the board too much, because I was trying to represent a made straight and I was pretty sure he had a set or two pair, something along those lines.

We were both pretty deep. I had like 300,000 more, he had like 200,000-something more—it would have hurt if I went all-in and he called.

On the river, he checked, I shoved all-in, and he folded pretty quickly.

I showed my bluff. That was strictly an emotional thing—I was so wound up and happy that I got out of this miserable trap that I put myself in and glad to have all of these chips. It was a stupid thing to show the bluff, but I was proud of myself!

And that's when I felt like people started talking about me in a good way. Like I'm not such a fish anymore. I'm a lunatic and you might want to leave me the fuck alone.

Phil Hellmuth: I was on top of my game. I won two bracelets in '03. I was in the zone. Going into that Main Event, I was pretty sure there was going to be a deep run for me.

I made the deep run, but then I was running really bad from 36 down to 28 players. And at 27, we re-drew to a new table, three tables left. Sammy Farha was at my table now. So was Jason Lester. I got into a hand with Jason Lester that everyone's seen on TV.

Sammy Farha opened. Jason Lester moved in. I'm in the big blind with two queens and I studied forever. The video doesn't show how long I studied, because this is a huge decision. I have to put like 170,000 of my 230,000 or so in the pot. And it's one of those situations where I'd like to fold, because I feel like I can just move my chips up effortlessly from there.

I'd watched Jason Lester play at my table that day. I'd seen him move all-in with kings twice and it just didn't have the same feel. I knew it wasn't aces, I was pretty sure it wasn't kings, and I started to think, *He has jacks.* So I called him and when he flipped up jacks, you can just see it in my eyes, I say, "Jacks, that's exactly what I thought you had," or something like that.

I mean, I made an amazing world-class read on Jason. If I win that hand, I'm going to have like 400,000 in chips. I'm going to cruise into the final 18. And who knows what will happen? I may have won it. When you win two bracelets, both in hold 'em, in one year, and now you're deep in the Main Event, I felt like if I won that hand I was going to be there right at the end.

Instead, he hits a jack on the river.

Then, to add insult to injury, you deal me A-K the next hand, and I don't even remember who busted me [Tomer Benvenisti], but whoever the guy was, he never even thought about folding tens. If he would have had tens and I would have had kings, he's just going to give me all his chips; he didn't even think about it. But he calls and I lose. The chances of me losing both of those hands are about 9-1.

Dave Swartz: The first time I really started taking notice of Chris Moneymaker was through his confrontations with Dutch Boyd. Dutch was one of these interesting characters who caught our eye early on. He had some quote in one of the early telecasts, something along the lines of, "Poker is a lot like sex. Everybody thinks they can do it, but nobody really knows what they're doing."

Dutch Boyd: I'm going to take credit for that line. But I think the first time I ever heard that line, or something to that effect, was a book by Andy Bellin called *Poker Nation*. I don't think it was word-for-word the same thing, but it was the same idea. He was writing about stuff he heard around the poker room.

Look, I'm sure people have said that same thing about golf. It just happens to be my quote, because in the editing room, when ESPN was sitting there going over a two-hour interview, they pulled that line.

So now, when people think about that quote, they think about me saying it. And I'll take it. But it didn't come to me on the spot.

Swartz: Dutch was this guy who had a presence about him and stood out.

In terms of how character development and coverage evolved, you went in with a game plan, and then you discovered people along the way. Dutch was one of the people we discovered along the way.

Boyd: The night before my interview with ESPN, I was really thinking about how it would appear on TV. I knew they were looking for little sound bites that were going to look good on TV. I needed to make sure I had long pauses between little sound bites, give them as many five- and ten-second sound bites as I can, and try to make their job really easy. I thought if I can just make their job easy, I'm going to get a lot more coverage than I deserve.

And I did. I got a lot more coverage than I deserved.

Prior to winning my first bracelet in 2006, I probably had the highest fame-to-results ratio of any poker player in the world. It's two different skills. You have Phil Ivey, who's one of the best poker players in the world, and how many minutes did he get on ESPN in 2003? It's like he wasn't even there. But talking to the media and doing interviews is a totally different skill than knowing if your opponent's going to check-raise bluff.

Farha: Dutch Boyd was aggravating me so much. Every hand, he says the word "raise" and looks at each player in the eyes, one by one, and takes about five minutes to say how much he's going to raise.

I like to play fast, and it gets aggravating when you see a player like this. TV doesn't show that.

Boyd: I was playing with Moneymaker for the first time on Day Four. I asked him what he did and he said he was an accountant in Tennessee. I asked how he got there and he said he won his way in. And he introduced me to his friend David Gamble. And he introduced me to his dad. They all seemed like good guys, good old boys.

He wasn't really very talented at poker; it didn't really seem like he belonged there. It seemed like he was kind of winging it. But anyone can win.

Anyway, we'd been playing for about three hours and I got a pretty good tell on him. He was the kind of player who was very aggressive and if you checked to him, he was going to bet. All the time. And he had something, almost like out of a Hollywood movie, where he would flare his nostrils when he was weak. It was like a bunny, man.

So I was like, *This is going to be so easy to play against this guy. I love having him to my left. All I gotta do is check to him and let him bet, and I'll just look at his nostrils, and if they start flaring up, I'll come over the top of him.* And that's what I did in our big famous hand.

Moneymaker: The flop was 9-5-2 and I had pocket

threes. Dutch had me covered and he raised me all-in. I was sort of in the zone at that point. There's no easy way to describe that.

My first instinct was that he had two overcards. I really couldn't see him shoving in with a set there.

Pre-flop, he bet and I called, and when I called, I remember he shot me a look like, *Oh crap, what the hell are you doing in my pot?* It was more of a concerned look than a confident look. It's hard to describe. But I really felt like he didn't have a whole lot and when he did the check-raise all-in, I just couldn't put him on a hand that he was going to risk basically his tournament life on. I figured, *He has complete air and it's a move.*

Boyd: I didn't really think too far ahead as far as what specific hand he was weak with. I just was thinking, *He's weak, so come over the top.* The chances of me going broke that hand were zero percent. And I really just felt like he was not going to make the call. I saw the little tell that I was waiting for and I made the move.

Moneymaker: I couldn't see him doing that with an A-9. I think he calls with A-9; I don't think he shoves.

So I went through my head, trying to figure out what he could have, and my first gut instinct is he has A-K, A-Q. It turned out it was K-Q. But I was even thinking, *If he has A-K, A-Q, and he catches an ace, then I have four more outs to catch a straight on the river, so if I'm right and he does suck out, at least I can re-suck out.*

So I called and said, "Low cards, dealer!" I wanted people to know before Dutch showed his cards that I knew where I was when I made this pretty sick call.

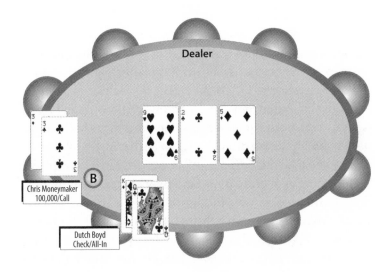

Swartz: I remember Dutch shaking his head and saying, "That's a heck of a call, Moneymaker."

Moneymaker: Jason Lester said to me that it was one of the best calls he'd ever seen. He might have meant that it was one of the worst calls he'd ever seen, but at the time, I thought it was a compliment. He could have meant it the complete opposite way and I was just too inexperienced to realize it.

Boyd: A lot of people are like, "Amazing call, Chris!" But I didn't think it was amazing at all. I thought his call was pretty bad, honestly.

Even if I was bluffing there, I could easily be bluffing with better. And when I'm not, it's not like there's any rule against one of my overcards hitting. Or the board double-pairing and him being counterfeited.

He put himself in a bad spot. He put himself in a position to go broke. And you just don't want to do that in poker tournaments. He was ahead, so you can't really fault the guy for putting his money in when he's ahead. But at the same time, he did make a mistake getting all of his chips in with two more cards to come when he's not *that* much ahead. Even in the best-case scenario, which it turns out he was actually in, he's still eliminated, what, 30% of the time? You don't really want to put yourself in those positions. But that's his fearlessness showing up. He didn't know what that 30% feels like.

You hear all the time about people getting it in with aces in the Main Event and losing. And they complain about how unlucky they were. "Oh, I'm supposed to win that 85% of the time." What people don't really talk about is all the hands that led up to somebody else having you covered. They don't talk about the six or seven times before where they got all their chips in with aces and it held up.

You only really need to be all-in with aces three times before you're a 'dog to win all three. You're parlaying. If you keep getting all of your chips in, it's just a matter of time before you go broke.

Chris was all-in against me. Seventy percent of the time, he wins. Thirty percent of the time, the *whole* poker world is different.

Swartz: For him to make that call for his tournament life was really incredible. With pocket threes, you're dead against any pair four and above and even if it's just overcards, you're only a slight favorite. Most professionals would lay down pocket threes in that situation every day.

But Chris just played the game differently. He wasn't a professional. He might not have known what was the "right" play at the time. He just went with his gut. And it worked for him.

He was playing the game differently—in large part because he *was* different.

Greg Raymer: What Chris has never been given credit for, he's one of the best hold 'em players I've ever seen when it comes to putting someone else on a hand. That's Phil Hellmuth's great talent. Phil is better at it than anyone I've ever played with. But Chris is right up there near the top. And Chris was great at it back when he was a raw talent in '03.

But he didn't have a great feeling for the math of poker and basic strategy. The hand against Dutch Boyd, it was a great call, but the problem with that call is that it was a wet enough board that even if you're correct that he's bluffing, you still might only be 50% for your hand to hold up. It was a great read, but you could still argue that, if you know all the mathematical possibilities, it was incorrect to call for your tournament life.

Farha: Chris Moneymaker calls all-in with pocket threes and the funny part, he made statement, "Come on, dealer, give me two low cards," without looking at Dutch Boyd's hand. He knew pocket threes was the best, and it was!

I'm watching this and I'm laughing to myself! Where do they come from, that they play like this? This is not poker.

Boyd: One thing that I really regret doing was going all-in. I feel like if I would have re-raised the minimum, or re-raised like 2½ times his bet, it would have looked a lot less like a bluff.

Hey, he made a good read. But I could have been trying to push him around with fours. Or sevens. There's a lot of hands there where I could actually be ahead and *feel* weak. There's a lot of hands there where I could be ahead and just want to shut the hand down. I think that if I have sixes or sevens there, it makes just as much sense. A-5 makes sense there. I could go through and list every possible hand I could have, but I had K-Q. So I had the overcards. He was right. He makes the call. And he fades the overcards.

Goldman: That was a turning-point hand. The hand with Dutch gave Chris the confidence to go with his reads and the confidence that he actually had some game. I think that up until that point, he wasn't really sure that he was a contender.

Boyd: I told him about his nostrils tell after I was eliminated. Why not? But I don't think he believed me. He probably still doesn't believe that he did that. That's okay. He can think what he wants. I'll think what I want.

Moneymaker: Dutch Boyd told me about that tell after he busted from the tournament. But I don't know if it was an accurate tell or not. To be honest, for the first three or four days, I never really bluffed, so my nostrils were never really flaring.

Boyd: It's easy to think that you're the best player in the room. But there's a lot of good players. I believe that my confidence led to my eventual downfall against Moneymaker and then my elimination hand against Farha. I feel like I got a little too confident.

Farha: Dutch Boyd went all-in on a flop that had an ace and a queen. I had A-9. I decided to call him. If he had me, he had me. But it made no sense for him to go all-in if he has a monster hand. The situation said to me he couldn't beat A-9 or else he wouldn't have gone all-in. He had Q-J and I knocked him out of the tournament.

Boyd: When I got eliminated, I was conscious of the fact that no one wants to see me busting out of this thing winning $100,000 and complaining. No one's going to feel bad for the guy who wins half a million dollars, then exits in tears. We've seen that over and over, when people get knocked out, and they only win $40,000, and they feel crushed, and they cry. But the people at home are thinking, *Man, I work a year and don't make that much money.*

So I decided to really put on a good face. I was going to make it look like I was excited with what I won, rather than disappointed. And when I think about all the acting I've ever done in poker, that was the best. Because I was *not* feeling happy at that moment. When I got knocked out, I felt like I'd been hit with a hammer.

People saw that on ESPN and they ask me, "Why were you so happy?" Well, it's because the cameras were there.

The fact is, it still hurts, thinking about how close I came. I might never come that close to winning the championship event again.

When you're deep in the Main Event, it's almost like you're living a dream. It feels like fate. It's predetermined, and you're going to win it, and nothing's going to stand in your way. The universe wants you to win. It wasn't until I was out the door that I realized the universe doesn't care.

Lederer: I have never been able to hang around a tournament I got knocked out of—certainly not one that mattered to me. I just have to get out of there. I have no interest in going back and watching the final table. It just hurts too much. Those are my chips they're playing with.

In 2003, I got eliminated on Day Four, in 19th place. I didn't want to get out of bed for a week. I just knew, 19th place, I was really sniffing it, I was really playing well. That elimination was the most disappointing and devastating elimination of my poker career.

Remember, I'd finished fifth in 1987, before I even knew

what that meant. And now here's my first chance to come back to the final table, there are cameras there, the game is changing, I'm playing the best poker I've ever played—I'd won a couple of WPTs within the past year. I mean, I'm really sharp. And it just felt extremely winnable.

I may not have known it then, but I felt it, that that might be my last chance in the Main Event. And that's a sad thing. I knew there were going to be even more people the next year. I knew 2003 was the last year in my life that I'm ever going to have an opportunity to win the Main Event by beating only 800 people. Now you show up and I don't care who you are and how optimistic you are, the idea of believing you'll win the Main Event is just ridiculous.

When I started, that was a realistic career goal: "I'm going to win the Main Event someday." When I finished fifth, it was, "Okay, I'll be back again at the final table. I'll have another shot at this." Now it's not a tournament you can expect to win or that you really have on your list of career goals.

So there was a real sadness when I got eliminated in '03 that I haven't experienced since and hadn't experienced before.

Hellmuth: After being busted, I was completely inconsolable.

I remember the ESPN cameras following me down the street. I was walking toward the Golden Nugget from the Horseshoe, and TV cameras were following me and trying to get an interview, and I was inconsolable. I felt like knocking stuff over, throwing stuff. I was in pain, because I felt like I deserved better.

I just remember thinking, *I don't need cameras in my face right now.* It was only later that I realized it was probably good to give an interview when I'm mad.

Goldman: When we got down to 16 players or so, we had two PokerStars players left, Chris and Olof Thorson. And Olof Thorson was chip leader.

I'd been up all day, watching the World Series, and I needed to go get a cup of coffee, so I left, knowing that Chris was in about seventh or eighth place and Olof was chip leader by a pretty decent margin. So I went over to Starbucks. I was gone maybe 15 minutes. And by the time I came back, Olof was out.

It turns out there was one key hand that he got involved in with Amir Vahedi. Amir had Q-8 suited and Olof had A-K, and they got involved in this big war. Amir flopped a flush draw. Olof made an incredible read and believed he was on a flush draw. All the money went in with Olof holding ace-high and Amir actually had a lot of outs. He had 15 outs. Amir paired up on the river and that hand crippled Olof.

One or two hands later, Olof picks up pocket kings and gets involved in another gigantic pot with Sammy, in which Sammy has A-J. Flop comes ace-high, Olof still moves all-in. Sammy snap-calls him and he's out.

Imagine you're the marketing guy at PokerStars and your dream has come true: There are 16 people left in the World Series and you've got two of them, including the chip leader! So now you feel like you can finally take a break, so you leave for a cup of coffee, and when you come back 15 minutes later, your key horse is walking away.

And now the only guy that you have left is this Money-maker character.

Matt Savage: Once we got down to the final 10 players—one elimination from the final table—we moved everyone to one table. But we only had nine cameras on the table. So two people had to share. That was awkward.

Moneymaker: I was playing snug as a bug in a rug when we got down to 10. I wanted to make the final nine. I didn't want to play another hand. I didn't care about being the one to bust somebody.

First of all, I just wanted to go to bed. It was 4 a.m. and I was tired as hell. But I just wanted to stay out of the way. I didn't want to get involved.

The only hand I played 10-handed was the A-Q against Ivey. If I played another hand, I don't remember it.

Lederer: Obviously, Chris Moneymaker is the big story to come out of that World Series of Poker.

But the next biggest thing that happened was the birth of Ivey. He had come close in 2002 and I remember him saying, "I'm going to win this thing in 2003," and I said, "Yeah, yeah," and there he was, where really he should have won that tournament. He was becoming the most intimidating tournament player in the world that year.

Moneymaker: Everybody thinks that I got lucky against Ivey. I didn't get lucky. I raised pre-flop with A-Q, Jason Lester had tens, Phil Ivey had nines, and they both flatted. The flop was Q-Q-6.

It came around to me and I bet 75,000. Ivey only had about 475,000 left.

Everybody says I bet too small to get him out of there— my bet size kept him around—but that's what I wanted to do. I didn't want to run people off when I have A-Q; that would be stupid.

Jason folded his tens, Ivey called with his nines.

And I didn't get lucky. I got very unlucky when he hit a two-outer. He hit a nine on the turn.

He checked to me, I bet 200,000, he raised 200,000 more

all-in, and obviously I'm never folding there. It's a cooler. I just got the better end of it when I hit an ace on the river.

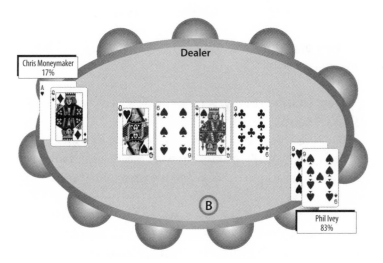

Dan Harrington: My reaction to that ace hitting was, "Oh, good." The money went to the right spot as far as I was concerned. That feeling was of unremitting joy.

Barry Greenstein: I got a call from Phil when he had just gotten knocked out, and he says, "You won't believe the hand I just played."

In those days, he used to always ask me about hands, because he really wasn't a no-limit player at that time; he was more of a seven-card-stud player who was transitioning into no-limit. And he called me up and asked me about the hand, and I remember telling him I would have folded on the flop.

He said, "I almost did. And then I just had this feeling to call."

He felt like he was the best player at the table, and part of the reason he called on the flop was that he felt he was going to make the right decision on the turn. Whether it's to fold on the turn or call if he feels Chris is bluffing, he just felt he had a good feel for what was going on at the table. So that was his reason for calling.

Then once the nine came on the turn, the hand pretty much played itself.

Ivey: That was a very, very tough hand. I drove back east after that hand.

I believe I received $80,000. That was the payout.

But I really, really wanted to win that tournament. That was just such a tough hand. When that ace came down, I was like, *Wow.*

So I ended up driving back east and had a lot of time to think about it. It was a 72-hour drive back to New Jersey, because I just didn't feel like flying. Once I got back, I was fine. I was ready to play again.

Dave Swartz: Phil Ivey was looked at as the next great poker player. If Phil had won that hand against Moneymaker, he would have been the chip leader going into the final table. You would have had the greatest player in the world as the chip leader. Instead, the cards didn't come down that way and Moneymaker ended up knocking out the most dangerous player in the game.

I often wonder, had Ivey won that hand and gone on to win the Main Event, would everything still have happened? You still would have been talking about a young kid, cool as cool could be, winning the Main Event. But would the poker boom have still happened the same way?

I don't know. Ivey didn't win his way in for $39 online and his last name wasn't Moneymaker.

Lederer: The hand where Moneymaker spikes the ace

and eliminates Ivey, that might have been one of the most important hands in poker history. It led to Moneymaker winning and the whole Moneymaker Effect, but it also kept Ivey from winning the Main Event, in my opinion.

I think if that hand goes the other way, it changes history enormously.

Moneymaker: People ask at what point I started thinking I was destined to win. I'd say it goes back to when I hit the eight on the turn against Humberto. That's when I was like, *Whoa, damn, I can win this thing.*

By the time the A-Q against Ivey rolled around, I was already pretty confident that I was going to win or get second.

I didn't know any better.

Shulman: Moneymaker busted Ivey and Chan. When you first start playing poker, that's what you think about, knocking people out. Being able to tell your friends, "Wow, I knocked out Johnny Chan. I knocked out Phil Ivey."

Side Action

Dutch Boyd: Even if I hadn't doubled up Moneymaker, I don't know that I would have gone on to win it. A lot of people still standing in the way were big threats.

Phil Ivey was the biggest threat once it got down to like 30 players.

Minh Nguyen, he's very good. I saw him as a huge threat.

I saw Jason Lester as a huge threat.

And I saw Amir Vahedi as a huge, huge threat.

Sammy Farha? Not so much. And Moneymaker? Not so much. If I was going to pick, when it was down to 20, who was going to come in first and second, those guys would not have been my pick. And those guys ended up taking all my chips between the two of them.

Still, whatever I might say or think about him as a poker player, Moneymaker is a stand-up guy. I really do like Chris. Every time I see him around, which sadly is not enough, every time I see him, I'm happy to see him. And anytime I'm not in the Main Event and he still is, I'll root for him to take it down.

Chapter 9

The Final Table

The biggest difference between the World Series of Poker Main Event now and in 2003, other than today's field sizes dwarfing the one Chris Moneymaker navigated, is in the execution and presentation of the final table.

Starting in 2008, the WSOP restructured the tournament for the sake of television. Rather than letting the competition play out naturally, then airing it on TV months later with most viewers knowing the winner the whole time, World Series organizers introduced the "November Nine" concept: The final table would be determined during the summer and play would be halted; ESPN would air its many weeks of Main Event coverage; and the final table would be contested as a major live(ish) event in November. During that roughly four-month break, all nine finalists would have a chance to become media darlings and pursue major sponsorship deals, and the public would (a) be more familiar with all nine players by the time the final table aired, and (b) watch the final table on ESPN in (almost) real time as eight players were eliminated and the champion was crowned.

It was a highly controversial decision.

Opposition arose against the November Nine innovation, as it does to almost any change. Traditionalists insisted that giving players four months to prep for the final table disrupted the natural order and flow of a poker tournament. There was also the question that nobody wanted to have to answer: What happens if one of the nine players dies during the interim? Morbid, certainly, but not an unrealistic scenario.

The November Nine concept moved forward despite the protests and it has now become part of the cultural fabric of the World Series of Poker. It's no longer considered controversial. It has become the new natural order of things. And it's made the 10th-place finisher every year's single most devastated bubble boy.

But in '03, there was no four-month gap. Given how late in the day (or, more accurately, early in the morning) it was when Phil Ivey was eliminated in 10th place, players were lucky if they could manage four hours of sleep. Ivey was out, the remaining nine spent a few moments celebrating that they'd all be earning six figures, and the focus quickly shifted to the work ahead of them that afternoon and evening.

Thanks in part to the massive pot he won when he eliminated Ivey, Moneymaker brought 2,344,000 in chips to the final table, 28% of the chips in play. His closest competitor was Amir Vahedi with 1,407,000. Sammy Farha sat in third place with 999,000.

In fourth place was an amateur who might have inspired some degree of "Moneymaker Effect" if he'd won, a rotund expedition guide named Tomer Benvenisti who qualified for the Main Event in a $125 live satellite.

The rest of the final table was made up of relatively mild-mannered pros. In chip-count order: David Singer, Jason Lester, Dan Harrington, Young Pak, and David Grey. This being the pre-November Nine era, some of them were barely shown on TV and their roles in the 2003 Main Event, as far as the poker public is concerned, will forever pale in comparison to such players they outlasted as Ivey, Dutch Boyd, Howard Lederer, and Phil Hellmuth. How far you go in the tournament might be merit-based, but how much screen time you get is not. If you're quiet and/or don't get involved in any wild hands while at a table with hole-card cams, you're treated like a movie extra. As a result, the accomplishments of a few of the men who made the most famous final table ever played were completely forgotten soon thereafter.

In this chapter, naturally, we hear quite a bit from final-table competitors Moneymaker, Farha, and Harrington.

Among those who didn't have a seat at the table, but weigh in with their recollections, are:

- Lou Diamond, the handicapper and ESPN production assistant who somehow predicted the Moneymaker win on Day One;
- Matt Savage, the second-year WSOP tournament director;
- Nolan Dalla, the Horseshoe public-relations director;
- Kenna James, who was eliminated from the tournament on Day Four;
- Fred Christenson, a senior director of programming for ESPN;
- Norman Chad, the ESPN color commentator;
- and Brian Koppelman, the co-writer of *Rounders*, the movie that first introduced Chris Moneymaker to no-limit hold 'em.

"I felt like I was on steroids."

Lou Diamond: I wish I could have bet on Chris back on Day One or Day Two. But that year, it wasn't available until the final table, so unfortunately, I only got 3-to-1 on him, because he had all the chips. And there was a $100 or $200 limit on it.

Matt Savage: Even though Moneymaker was the chip

leader, people were not thinking he had a chance. It was a tough table. Nobody expected that chip lead to hold up.

Sammy Farha: The table was tough. You have Jason Lester, Dan Harrington, David Grey, Amir Vahedi. Chris Moneymaker was the only one who wasn't tough. Nobody paid attention to him, because who cares? When you have one bad player, you don't focus on him as much.

Nolan Dalla: I thought it was going to be Amir Vahedi's year. That was my pick. Jason Lester didn't have a lot of chips, but he had the pedigree to win. And then Dan Harrington—how do you not count him among the contenders if he's at the final table?

Sammy Farha was interesting in that everyone knew Sammy was very close to Benny Behnen, and I remember Benny was hoping Sammy would win, because he figured Sammy would take the $2.5 million and go downstairs and gamble it all away. That's what Benny was rooting for. He thought this was going to be good for the Horseshoe if Sammy won. But really, Sammy wasn't the favorite at that table, because no-limit hold 'em wasn't Sammy's game; Omaha was his game. So this was not his element. I don't think Sammy was regarded, as a hold 'em player, on the level of Dan Harrington or Amir Vahedi.

Meanwhile, Moneymaker, out of the entire group of nine players, even though he had the chip lead, I don't think a lot of eyes were on him. He was not the focus, given the magnitude of the other personalities that were there.

Chris Moneymaker: Once the final table started, I knew I'd be heads-up with either Amir or Sammy at the end. Amir was, in my eyes, the craziest person at the table. Sammy was the second craziest.

So I told my dad the night before that Amir and Sammy are going to play a big pot together, they're gonna clash, and whoever wins that clash, I'm going to play heads-up for the title.

Dalla: Amir took over the chip lead from Moneymaker early at the final table. Then he just imploded. He completely self-destructed in a ridiculous bluff and, unfortunately, that's how Amir Vahedi is largely remembered now, for a destructive bluff where he ruined any chance he had of winning. To watch that, if you're a friend of Amir Vahedi, I still look at that and cringe.

Dan Harrington: It's easy to call it a meltdown, but I don't look at it that way. A lot of the theorists, as far as what's the proper strategy when you have ascending order of payouts and what kind of chances you're supposed to take, they would not agree with what Vahedi did—and I put myself in that camp.

On the other hand, it's high volatility and you do get rewarded if you succeed. You have a good chance to win the tournament. So it's not an unreasonable strategy.

Farha: I never played with Amir before; 2003 was the first time. And I only played with him on one table before the final table.

That one hand, I flopped top set. I was surprised that he was bluffing. But I guess he thought, *It's Sammy Farha, he's aggressive, let me see if I can get him out. I'm more aggressive than him.* A lot of players think that way.

I was fortunate to get paid off with a full house, that the guy decided to bluff there.

Harrington: Vahedi got to where he was in the tournament because he took chances at key times. So he picked a flop where it didn't rate that his opponent had a hand. He kept betting into Sam Farha, and Sam had a flopped set of nines, and Sam played the hand very well, played it cozy. He knew what Vahedi was about, that Vahedi was going to try to take him off the hand.

It was unfortunate for Vahedi that he was up against Sam Farha, because Sam has the reputation that he'd call the flop with nothing to try to take away the hand from Vahedi. Vahedi would be on his guard against someone else if they called on the flop; against another opponent, he might have stopped right away. But against Farha, Farha could have taken a card to try to take the hand away from him, so Vahedi continued to try to bluff him. He got unlucky in that regard.

Maybe Vahedi wasn't supposed to pick on Sam to make that kind of play against. But Vahedi made his living doing that.

Moneymaker: That's what Amir Vahedi did the whole tournament. I played with him for 2½ days, and that's the way he played.

I mean, he moved all-in with a Q-8 against Olof Thorson's A-K on Day Four and said, "You gotta have balls, baby!" and stands up and starts cheering. That's what he did the whole time.

He was pushing very very thinly. He was making very risky plays. He was very aggressive. It's how he got his chips and ultimately how he lost them.

Kenna James: I was part of a team that was being sponsored and Amir Vahedi was one of the other members on the team. I went to dinner with Amir the night before the final table.

People assume Amir's collapse at the final table was devastating to him, but Amir was never devastated. Amir Vahedi played a fearless game. In fact, one of his quotes was, "In order to live, one must be willing to die." He played fearlessly. He was willing to look like he was falling apart, because that was his game. Oftentimes, it worked. But when it didn't, he looked really bad.

Savage: His collapse happened so quickly. In real time, it took about two or three hours for him to go from chip leader to busted.

Fred Christenson: The charm of the World Series of Poker was you played until somebody won. You play overnight, you play until the sun comes up, you play until somebody caves in and somebody wins.

Savage: We played longer days than we planned to, because we had more players than we expected. So exhaustion was definitely a part of it.

Norman Chad: As the final table wore on, we heard so many stories about how Sammy Farha had played all night the night before—and he had. As these semi-degenerate poker players do, they can't get away from a good cash game. So he played the tournament the night before until 3 or 4 o'clock in the morning, then he played in a cash game all morning, and then he's playing for the world championship the next day.

Farha: For five days, I had no sleep. None. I did not sleep. And the last day, the reason I lasted, I drank 20 Red Bulls, about 20 cups of coffee. I could not function.

Harrington: I've played a lot of different games—chess,

backgammon, whatever—where you had to put in long grueling hours. If you get down near the end where victory depends on you being alert, even when I'm tired, I could dig down and I could get something out of myself to give that final push.

Well, at the final table, for the first time in my life, I dug down and there was *nothing* there. I hit the wall. I couldn't come up with a coherent strategy.

Here's how bad it was. When it got down to three-handed, me, Sammy, and Chris, I wanted to bet 75,000, which was the right bet for that situation. And I sat there and I couldn't calculate how to make the 75,000-chip bet. I had a whole bunch of 25,000 chips in front of me and I *could not* figure out how to get to 75,000. It was an insurmountable problem.

Moneymaker: For the first part of the final table, I was on cruise control. I didn't play many pots; I didn't want to get involved. My plan was to sit back and let other people eliminate themselves until it got short-handed.

Then, honestly, I don't know what happened when we got three-handed. I just started raising every single hand. I was just destroying both of them with aggression, to the point where Sammy's like, "Let's just go home. I'm done. This is really not fun anymore."

I turned into mini Stu Ungar. I was just crushing them. I felt like I was on steroids. I was playing in a perfect zone. I bluffed every hand, raised every hand, no one was putting up a fight, I was just dwindling them down.

They were both really tired. I was full of energy and people in the crowd could tell that I was just running them over.

Harrington: I didn't employ the right strategy at all. Being dead tired, I was very passive, which is an incredible blunder to make in those situations. I've written books on how to play in those situations and I certainly didn't follow that advice there; I was just too tired to.

When it was just the three of us left, Sam Farha was sleeping at the table, I was dead on my feet, and Chris Moneymaker was over there bouncing around like this was the greatest thing since sliced bread. And I was thinking, *We got no chance under these conditions. I mean, we just don't have a chance. This kid loves being here, has the energy, and Sam and I just want to go to sleep somewhere.*

Moneymaker: I was just going with the flow. I picked up some cards, then I just kept raising even when I didn't have cards. And I sensed that they were tired. They weren't really playing back at me at all. So I kept raising more, putting more pressure on them, and everything was working, and I felt like they couldn't hurt me.

I was in the zone and in one of those special moments you don't get in poker very often.

Brian Koppelman: Isn't that what's so magical about the game of poker? That if you are somehow in the matrix, if you're able to lock in, and you can see that clearly for a short period of time, you can have streaks of brilliance.

Harrington: After I busted in third place, ESPN asked me for a prediction, and I told them, "No one over 40 is ever going to win this tournament again." The average age of the winners has since gone down to the high 20s.

I remember being in Ireland a few years ago and there were three people left in the tournament. The youngest guy won, the middle-aged one came in second, and the oldest came in third. By the way, their ages were 21, 24, and 26.

That's really what it's turned into. It's become an endurance contest.

At the Main Event in 2004, I was at the final table again. I was sitting next to a younger player, and he nudged me and said, "I know you tell everyone how brutal it is on you to get down to this point in the tournament; you don't have the energy anymore. Well, I'm 28, and it's brutal on me too."

Side Action

Phil Hellmuth: I stopped by the final table, just to see who was left.

There was Sammy Farha, who put a bad beat on me earlier in the event.

And I saw this kid, Moneymaker. I think they were six-handed. He was like, "Phil"—I mean, they were actually playing, he threw his hand away, he came over, he was like, "Hey, can I get an autograph?" I thought it was pretty cute, he asked for an autograph from me.

Here's a guy trying to win $2.5 million, he's in the middle of a final table, and he stops play just to come ask me for an autograph.

So I signed something for him, and I said, "Go get 'em. Try to win it." That's what I told him.

Chapter 10

Heads-Up

"Heads-up poker may be the purest form of psychological warfare this game has to offer. It's no wonder why the old westerns and *Rounders* and every other poker movie always comes down to a one-on-one battle between the good guy and the villain."

That quote comes from David Williams, a poker pro who rose to prominence one year after Moneymaker's victory, when the young Texan finished runner-up to Greg Raymer in the 2004 WSOP Main Event. Williams may have lost his most notable heads-up match, but his understanding of the game is spot on: Heads-up is all about getting into the other guy's head, and it provides the ultimate in dramatic poker theater.

As the number of players at a table decreases, it becomes imperative that a player's aggression and activity increase. The blinds come around faster, so you simply have to play more hands. If you fold 18 hands in a row at a six-handed table, you've lost 50% more in blinds than you would have in 18 deals at a nine-handed table.

When you're playing heads-up, you're in either the small blind or big blind *every hand*. The small blind has the button and acts first pre-flop and last on every subsequent street. Some pros will tell you that you should raise every single heads-up hand on the button pre-flop. A hand like K-6 offsuit, which you'd fold without hesitation in most nine-handed games, is a hand with which you'd raise without hesitation on the button heads-up.

The more players at the table, the more you can pick and choose with whom you tangle. Heads-up, there's nowhere to hide. So if you're folding too often and too easily, you're ceding control and handing your opponent confidence and momentum—and when you only have one opponent, that's an almost insurmountable problem.

Heads-up poker is about putting your opponent to the test and doing everything you can to get inside his head. In every heads-up match, you continually feel like Vizzini in *The Princess Bride* trying to figure out which cup contains the poisonous iocane powder. You must consider what your opponent thinks you have and what he thinks you think he has— then possibly go a step or two beyond that. If you're going to play A-B-C poker, the only way you'll win a heads-up match is by getting hit by the deck. In order to win with average luck, you have to be unpredictable, flexible, and focused.

With all this in mind, understanding that heads-up favors the seasoned, aggressive, versatile player, it's not surprising that most observers considered Sam Farha the favorite to beat Chris Moneymaker when their heads-up match began. The amateur held nearly a 2-1 chip lead, with almost 5.5 million to Farha's 2.9 million. But did the kid from Tennessee know how to play heads-up poker? And even if he did, could he hold up under the pressure that Farha was sure to put on him?

Those were the questions buzzing about Benny's Bullpen after Moneymaker scored his fifth elimination of the day, taking out Dan Harrington in third place. And it wouldn't be long before everyone in attendance would witness what probably remains, more than a decade later, the greatest hand in televised poker history.

Unsurprisingly, nearly everyone interviewed for this book had something to say about the Moneymaker-Farha heads-up match and what has since become known as "The

Bluff of the Century," or, to some, simply "The Bluff." In Chapter 10, you'll of course hear plenty from Moneymaker and Farha, but you'll also hear from:

- Moneymaker's dad, Mike;
- Chris' good friend and backer, David Gamble;
- 441 Productions' Matt Maranz and Dave Swartz;
- ESPN color commentator Norman Chad;
- Binion's Horseshoe PR Director Nolan Dalla;
- WSOP Tournament Director Matt Savage;
- PokerStars VP of Marketing Dan Goldman;
- *Rounders* co-writer Brian Koppelman;
- the man who was first to predict a Moneymaker win, Lou Diamond;
- and poker pros and ambassadors of the game Daniel Negreanu, Mike Sexton, and Erik Seidel.

"When you see this on ESPN, you are going to see the best bluff in the history of the World Series of Poker."

Chris Moneymaker: I felt like I was going to win. I was really confident—and then they brought out two and a half million dollars and put it on the table in front of me.

It started to sink in, what we were playing for. That is a lot of fuckin' money.

David Gamble: When they brought that money up the escalator and they walked over with shotguns and armed guards and they dumped that money on the table, Chris turned his hat around, and he came over to us, and he was breathing *hard*.

Moneymaker: The stress really kicked in when I saw the money. It messed with my head a little bit.

I started thinking maybe Sam and I need to talk a deal here, because now that they put this money in front me, maybe it would be smart for me to go ahead and guarantee myself like $1.6 million or $1.8 million and not have to play under a ton of stress.

So I said to Sammy, "Let's leave the table and go to the bathroom."

We walked into the bathroom and I said, "You want to split the money evenly and play for the bracelet?"

Sammy's response was, "Instead, we can put it all together—the $1.3 million and the $2.5 million—and play for the whole thing." Like winner takes all.

And I'm like, "Ha ha, very funny." At the time, I thought he was joking. But knowing Sammy now, he probably wasn't.

He said, "In all seriousness, I have more experience. I think I need a little bit more." Like I should give him more than an even split.

I'm like, "Dude, I got you 2-to-1 in chips! Are you crazy?"

He's like, "I think I need more."

So I'm like, "We're playing it out then, straight up," and that was the end of it.

Him thinking he deserved more, that really pissed me off and made me want to crush him.

Sammy Farha: I was in the bathroom. I said, "What do you want, Chris?"

He said, "Let's chop it."

I said, "No, chopping is not fair."

He said, "Give me an offer, I'll do whatever."

I said, "Well, I don't want to embarrass you with my offer."

That's exactly what happened.

Honestly, I knew I'm making a mistake, but it's an ego

thing. It's a stupid thing. Even though I'm so tired, I figured this kid can't beat me, even if I die on the table.

Mike Sexton: I've been around long enough to realize it doesn't matter what kind of novice that guy is and what kind of experienced player you are. If he's got a big chip lead on you and the guy wants to chop it 50-50, I'm going for the 50-50. He can't be all that bad if he got that far, through almost a thousand players.

But Sammy thought he could beat him and Sammy didn't need the money that much. He thought it might put more pressure on Moneymaker if he had to play for the money. Sammy thought he might crack.

Erik Seidel: I thought it was a crazy super-nice offer for Sammy, and I was surprised he wasn't taking it. Moneymaker may have been an amateur, but he was a crafty guy, and you couldn't spot him that big a lead.

They were on a little break and I said to Moneymaker that I would take his side of that for $100,000, basically offering him insurance. But he had no idea who I was. So to him, he's dealing with just some random person who came over to him, and it's unfortunate for me that he didn't know me, because it seemed like a great bet for me.

I think he said something like, "Well, maybe you should talk to my dad."

Dave Swartz: Watching Chris Moneymaker and Sammy Farha go heads-up, it was out of a movie script.

You had the established pro who had the look and feel of everything you ever thought poker was, going up against this kid with the crazy name who by all historical data had no business being there.

Brian Koppelman: Even re-watching it now, you're sure Sammy Farha's going to win! How's he going to beat Sammy?

Nolan Dalla: I'm standing right behind Moneymaker, maybe 10 feet away, as they're getting ready to start playing heads-up. And George Fisher comes up, taps me on the shoulder, and he whispers to me—I'll never forget his words—he said, "It's over."

I turn to him. "What are you talking about?"

He says, "He's got no chance. No shot. It's over."

I'm like, "What do you mean?"

He says, "Sammy is going to destroy him."

And I'm right by the table, this conversation is being whispered, so I can't start arguing. I just have to stand there and nod and say, "Okay."

Norman Chad: All the way down to the finish, I never thought Chris had a chance to beat Sammy Farha. I had five days of watching him and then the final table, and I still didn't think he was going to win until he won.

Plus, I was rooting for Sammy Farha, because I was a moron. Nothing against Chris—I just had no idea that Chris Moneymaker winning was going to be the engine that drives the car in terms of the poker boom.

Matt Savage: I think people felt that if Sammy could win one big hand and get about even, it would be over for Chris.

Moneymaker: I knew Sammy's game plan going into heads-up. The conversation in the bathroom helped me figure out what he wanted to do.

Sammy normally likes to play big pots; he likes to gamble it up. But I knew that if he thinks he's that much better than me, he's going to want to keep the pots smaller and use his experience to try to whittle me down and get back close to even, and then he might start applying the pressure.

At the start of heads-up, he wasn't going to want to do anything to risk his tournament life. He wanted to play small-ball poker as best he could, to use his experience. I knew what he wanted to do to me and I just was not going to let that happen.

So I went out there with a plan to make him uncomfortable—basically, make him play really big pots when I didn't think he had a powerful hand. And that's where the bluff came in with the king-high vs. his pair of nines. I didn't think he'd want to lose to an amateur and look like an idiot if I'm sitting there with the nut flush or something. That hand was totally derived from the conversation we had in the bathroom.

Matt Maranz: The bluff. That was a great hand and you knew it was a great hand as it was happening. Even now, 10 years after that, people still are talking about that as the single best hand in televised poker history.

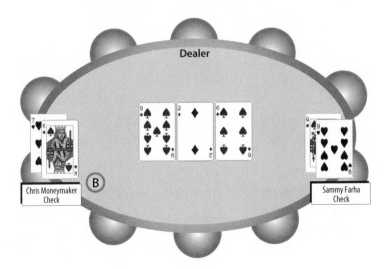

Moneymaker: I had K-7, Sammy had Q-9. The flop came 9-6-2 with two spades, and he checked the flop, and I think his plan was to check-call with top pair, because he didn't want to play a big pot against me. I think he was going to try to let me barrel at it; he was just going to check-call me all the way down.

And when I checked back to him, I don't know what he was thinking, but it was something out of the ordinary compared to what I'd been doing.

Farha: A good player, when he raises on the button pre-flop, he continues, on the flop, to bet. So I checked, and he checked on the button. Even though he raised pre-flop, he does not do a continuation bet.

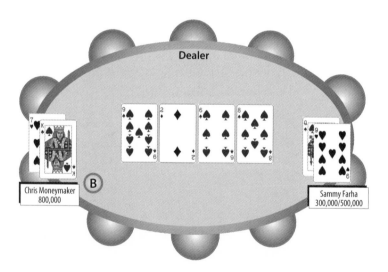

Moneymaker: The turn was the eight of spades. That gave me the second nut flush draw and an open-ended straight draw, and at this point, I'm ready to go. He bets, I raise, and if he wants to shove all-in, we're going to get the money in the middle.

Of course, I don't really want him to shove. I want him to fold.

When he calls me, I immediately think he has the ace of spades and like a six or seven in his hand. I really don't think he has a big made hand. I know he doesn't have a flush. But I think there's a good chance he can have a similar draw to what I have and I think he has the ace of spades.

So my plan on the river was to ship any river that was not a spade. If I made my straight, I was shipping. If I made my flush, I might just end up checking, because I did put him on the ace of spades—which would have been a really bad play, since he actually had the queen of spades. But my plan was to check any spade—unless, of course, it was the ace of spades—and go all-in on any other card. I was almost positive he didn't have a flush and almost positive he didn't have a straight and pretty sure he didn't have two pair. And I didn't think he could call me with anything other than those hands. It would even be a stretch for him to call me with two pair.

Savage: During that hand, on the turn, I made a mistake. Moneymaker put in his bet and I said, "Call."

Moneymaker immediately goes, "I said, 'Raise.'"

I could have screwed something up there. I could have changed history. That could have told Sammy something—maybe it did tell Sammy something!

So I felt really guilty about that and when I watch that now, I kind of cringe, because it could have made a difference.

But it was just me mishearing him. He didn't say it very loud. And the tension was really high, obviously.

Farha: On the turn, I bet, he raised. When he raised, I knew he was on the draw.

I don't want to go all-in, because if he misses, I know he's going to try to bluff me out and go all-in. And if he makes the hand, I'll know it and I won't lose another chip.

Moneymaker: At the end of the day, I bricked. The river was a blank, the three of hearts. And when I bricked, I went from being a little relieved, because I didn't want a spade to come, to being pissed off, because now I've got king-high and I've gotten myself in another one of these damned predicaments. But I went with Plan A. I said, "All-in." There was no Plan B if he called.

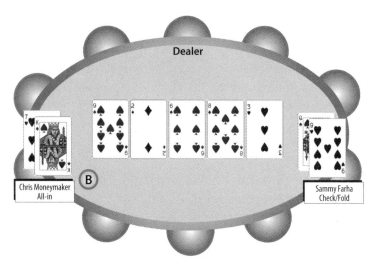

Chad: It's shot terrifically. It's an unbelievable hand. Chris has those sunglasses on where he's trying to be a statue. He doesn't want to give anything away.

Moneymaker: I remember that Amir talked with Sam in

a hand earlier in the day and the second that Amir said something, Sam called.

So when Sam started talking, I just told myself to sit there, shut up, shut your eyes, imagine you're on a beach, don't talk to him, don't give him any information, just be a statue. Don't move. If you don't give up any information, he can't hurt you. So just sit there and be quiet. If you lose, you lose; you've still got chips. It's obviously a huge hand, but you're already a millionaire. All this stuff just racing through my head.

And all the while I'm thinking, *Just fold. Just fold.* I really did think he was going to fold. When I made the bet, I really felt like he was going to fold, and the longer it went, I felt like, *Damn, he's trying to talk himself into calling.*

He was getting tired, he didn't want this to go on forever, but he didn't want to look like an idiot calling off with just a pair. So he was trying to talk himself into finding a hand to call with.

I started to get a little bit worried that his exhaustion might make him make a loose call, because he wanted to get it over with.

Farha: It took me 20 minutes—you don't see it on TV—it took me about 20 minutes to muck my hand on the river. And the reason I mucked it is because I started talking to myself and I doubted myself.

You should follow your instinct. I did not follow my instinct. When you take a long time, you lose your instinct. And that's what happened.

My plan went perfect. I said he's gonna go all-in, he went all-in on the river, and he missed it, he missed his draw. But I changed my plan.

Savage: Sammy probably thought it over for about two or three minutes, which is an eternity when you're sitting there. I thought Chris had a hand. I didn't think he was bold enough to make that move without a hand. I guess Sammy thought the same thing.

Moneymaker: I think they basically captured it on TV, how long he took to fold. Two minutes to think about a poker move—that's an eternity. That was the longest I'd ever waited for someone to make a decision.

Dalla: There was dead silence. While Sammy was deciding what to do, there was great respect for the moment.

This was before Joe Hachem and the "Aussie Aussie Aussie, Oy Oy Oy" chants, so the crowds weren't rowdy. There weren't big cheering sections. Chris' cheering section was his dad and one or two friends. Sammy Farha had no cheering section. Really, cheering sections didn't exist at the time.

The spectators who were there were all poker aficionados who loved the game, loved being part of history. There were about 300 or 350 people in that room; that's how many people witnessed the most important moment in poker history.

So the atmosphere was almost like a chess match. The discussions were in hushed whispers. It was a more serious cerebral gallery than what you see today.

And at the time, not knowing the hole cards, nobody knew what a pivotal hand that was. It wasn't as though the crowd knew they were witnessing one of the top five poker hands in history. We didn't even know it was a bluff. We thought Sammy had probably made a good fold.

Mike Moneymaker: From my vantage point, I couldn't

really see the cards. Nolan looked over there and he came back and said, "There's three spades on the board."

When Chris went all-in, I said, "Nolan, guess who's got two more spades? It's not Sammy." I thought Chris had it.

Seidel: I remember thinking that he *could have been* bluffing, but I certainly wasn't thinking, *Boy, Sammy should put his chips in.* It was just a great play by Moneymaker. He had no fear.

That was a great World Series moment. You have a guy putting his entire tournament life on the line against one of the most seasoned pros in the world, and he's a rank amateur, and he gets away with it.

Daniel Negreanu: I think Farha felt like he's the better player, so why take any big risks and play a big pot with the guy when you're going to grind him down safely?

If I'd found myself in Sammy's situation, it makes total sense to just throw the hand away. There's no sense getting it in there.

Dan Goldman: I was sitting next to [2000 World Series of Poker Main Event champion] Chris Ferguson, who was doing statistics. I don't know if he was doing it for any kind of an official role, but he had a notebook and he wrote down the actions for every hand, along with some comments. At the point at which Chris [Moneymaker] moved in on the river and Sammy was struggling with this one-pair call, Chris Ferguson leaned over and said, "When you see this on ESPN, you're going to see the best bluff in the history of the World Series of Poker."

Of course, we watched the hand play out and we didn't find out what Chris had or what Sammy folded.

Later on, after everything was done and I had a chance to

talk to Chris [Moneymaker] very briefly, I said, "The hand with Sammy right before you won … "

He said, "I had stone nothing."

I went back to Chris Ferguson and said, "You were right." And I remember thinking, *I don't ever want to play poker with this guy.*

Chad: I don't remember exactly how I worded it on TV, but I was being half-serious when I called it "the bluff of the century," and I think I mentioned that we're only a couple years into the century, but what the heck. It's just a great bluff.

Farha: Let me tell you, it was the worst bluff of the year, but it worked out for one reason: I bluffed myself out.

Chad: I know one person who doesn't think it's the bluff of the century is Sammy Farha. He's talked to me since, kinda bothered by that hand and bothered by the fact that we said it was such a great bluff. He doesn't think it was a great bluff. He just thinks it was a mistake and he played it badly, and he gives no credit to Chris Moneymaker at all.

I don't want to say he's a sore loser, but Sammy has a certain arrogance about his level of poker ability, and part of that arrogance is that Chris was not in his league, poker-wise. So he just believes that he didn't put the hand together correctly and he fouled up because he was so tired.

Farha: The reason I lost is that I underestimated my opponent. I didn't care at the end, I was so tired. I couldn't focus.

Now, if I'm playing Dan Harrington, it's a different story. I would have probably won it, because I could have focused more. With Chris, I did not focus.

Dalla: Only one person was allowed to watch the feeds from the hole-card cameras.

Over in a corner of the Horseshoe, probably 60 or 70 feet away from the final table, behind a black curtain, with a Horseshoe security officer standing guard, is essentially Oz—the only person in the entire world who knows what both players have.

I don't remember his name, but he worked for 441 Productions. And he comes up after the whole thing and says, "You're not going to believe this. I just saw the most amazing bluff in poker history!"

I'm like, "What? Are you kidding me?"

Because everybody thought Chris had a big hand. Everybody assumed Sammy had made a great fold.

That guy telling us—that wouldn't happen today. Now you've got total isolation with the person or people who can see the hole cards. But this guy just *had* to tell somebody his secret, what he'd just seen.

Moneymaker: It ended the very next hand.

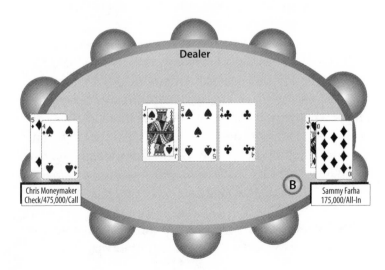

After I pulled that bluff off, I could tell he was agitated and I just thought, *Please, let me catch a big hand in the next five or six hands, and let him catch any piece of it, and I'm going to bust him.*

And it just so happens the very next hand, I flopped bottom two pair on a J-5-4 flop. I was thinking, *Please just give him a jack.*

He moved all-in and I knew he had a jack.

Farha: I had top pair and boom, he had bottom two pair. And he broke me.

So that tells you it was meant to be his.

You know, I made a mistake with one hand. I mucked top pair. And the next hand, I had top pair and I went all-in. So the first hand, people say, "Sammy, how could you muck top pair?" And the second hand, they say, "Why would you go all-in with top pair?"

You can't win either way.

Moneymaker: We got it all-in on the flop and waiting for those last two cards to come out, all I was thinking was, *Let's get it over with.*

At that point in my career, I didn't really know what a bad beat was. If that would have happened today, I would have been sweating a bad beat like a motherfucker.

But back then, it was my first live tournament and I didn't take any bad beats. That's why I won the tournament. I delivered one or two, but I never took any. When I got my money in good, I thought that was it. Waiting for the turn and river, it was a technicality. That's when poker was fun, when there was no such thing as a bad beat.

Mike Moneymaker: After he won, immediately, I ran down and we hugged. It was just spontaneous. And if you listen real good on TV, when we hugged, you could hear a crack.

He looked at me and said, "What was that?"

I said, "You owe me a pair of sunglasses, boy."

Moneymaker: All I remember saying to my dad is, "I did it."

There was so much emotion and so much going on, from the time I won until the time I got home, I don't really remember a whole hell of a lot.

I forgot I did an interview. I used to get so nervous doing interviews, I can't even believe I did it. I think I was so high on adrenaline. It was a surreal experience.

Goldman: In the interview session with the media after he won, one of the reporters asked him an incredibly stupid question, like, "Have you ever won this kind of money before?"

Chris held up a pack of hundred-dollar bills and he said, "I've never made *this* much money in a *year*."

Mike Moneymaker: Chris wanted me to go out partying, but I said, "Son, I'll see you at the airport tomorrow morning. I'm not 25 anymore. I'm going to the hotel and get some sleep."

He said, "Here, take the check."

I said, "Okay. I'll lock it up in the safe."

So they took me back, and Sammy was in the same limo. And he's sitting there with his $1.3 million in cash, in a liquor box, basically. Sammy was heading to the Venetian, I was heading to the MGM. And they dropped him off. They had two armed guards there to protect him.

Sammy made a comment that "your son's got a lot of class."

I said, "Thank you."

He said, "He came up to me and wished me good luck. Poker players don't do that and mean it, but he meant it. You can be proud of him."

To me, as a dad, that meant more than that he'd won the thing, Sammy saying that. He didn't have to say that.

Then he said, "I made one mistake. I thought he had the flush."

I said, "I thought he had it too. But could you take the chance that he didn't?"

He said, "No."

Farha: You might remember in 2005, the player who came in second was an amateur named Steve Dannenmann. He was sitting next to me at the table once, sometime after that. He said, "Sammy, I always wanted to ask you: Does it bother you, coming second? Because it's killing me now. At the time it didn't bother me, I was so happy to finish second. But now it's killing me. I missed all these endorsements."

I said, "Why do you think about it? You did well, it didn't bother you before, don't think about it now."

Finishing second, it does not bother me. To me, I'm looking at the money. Not at the title. The person I am, I don't think about yesterday. I made a lot of mistakes yesterday; I try to forget them, I move on. I can't survive if it's gonna bother me every day.

I'm gonna have a lot of swings. If I'm gonna be bothered by them, I better quit gambling or something.

Gamble: After Chris won, he grabbed that brick of cash, he gave me a bunch of hundreds, Bruce a bunch of hundreds. We gave everybody hundred-dollar tips, we were so excited.

Then we got in the ESPN limo and they took us out. We went out and just had a big ol' time. I just remember drinking a lot of beer. When it came to the end of the night, we were a little bit short on money.

Moneymaker: I think I brought out 15K, and I needed to borrow another 10K to cover our tab.

Lou Diamond: I was one of the gentlemen Chris was asking to get money from. I remember Chris going, "Lou, I need about 15." It was like three in the morning. I'm like, "I'm not that guy."

Gamble: We were able to call some poker buddies out of a poker game, guys who had some cash on them. They came over, gave us a short-term loan, and allowed us to get home.
They knew Chris was good for it.

Moneymaker: It was a fun night. [1996 world champion] Huck Seed was the one who helped me out. I was out of it. I don't remember much, but I do remember sitting there waiting for Huck to show up with the 10K.

Diamond: That night Chris gave me his sunglasses, the famous glasses. I had them in my car for a couple of years. Everybody's like, "Why don't you sell them on eBay or something?"
I couldn't do it. I'm like, "They're really Chris', that's his moment." So I'm like, "If I have the opportunity, I'm just going to give them back to him," and he was like, "Don't worry about it, Lou, you can have them."
But about two years later, he was down in the dumps, wasn't doing too good in tournaments, so I said, "Here, bring some luck back."
I gave him the glasses back and he started going on a tear.

Moneymaker: None of that is ringing a bell. I mean, I got pretty hammered that night I won. I think I lost them that night; I have no idea where they went. He might have swiped them, I don't know. They may have ended up in his possession. I don't really remember him giving them back to me, but it's been 10 years, so ...

Lon McEachern: I was dragging ass, because our work ended at the tournament probably at two in the morning. We had to shoot all of our on-cameras after the tournament was completed. So we were there for several hours afterward—probably as long as Chris was partying.

We finished and I had no idea where we were heading and how things were going to change. I was just hoping that my bank manager would let me off the next year to do the show again if we did it.

Side Action

Sammy Farha: A little while after he beat me, PokerStars came with a proposal for a rematch, and I said, "Yeah, I'll have the rematch." They wanted it to be for $20,000 or $40,000.

I said, "No, let's bring all the money we both won at the World Series and play for it!"

Dan Goldman: We put up, I think, $25,000 for an online rematch between Sammy and Chris in the fall of 2003. It was a charity event—it was understood that whoever won was donating their winnings to charity. It was a fairly slow-structure heads-up tournament.

Sammy is a delightful guy, but he barely knew how to use a computer. So getting him to agree to do this was a bit of a struggle, and getting the software installed and getting him up and running was a *big* struggle.

But we got him set up, and they played, and Sammy made quick work of him. It was not the epic struggle I was hoping for.

We had probably 20,000 people watching it online. We saw a pretty decent-sized spike in traffic for the couple of weeks after that, because we had people who tuned in just to watch the challenge match.

Farha: He played so bad. It went down fast. I mean, nobody will lose his money like this.

Chris Moneymaker: I don't think I played badly at all. It was an online tournament, and it was done in under 30 minutes, but that's not atypical of an online tournament.

Farha: I had A-10 of clubs, and I was so fortunate, I flopped a flush. I bet a little bit, he calls. By the river, there were four flush cards on the board. And he had the king. I bet. He went all-in. Tell me one beginning poker player who would go all-in! You want to call, it's okay. But how could you jeopardize all your money? You can't get called unless I have you beat, period. It was a bad play.

Moneymaker: I remember midway through the match, he won a big flip where I would have won the match if he hadn't won that flip. He won that flip and crippled me. I don't remember my bust-out hand. I have no recollection of the final hand or of me making a bad play. But I beat him when we had another rematch, a live one, at the World Series a couple years ago. I'll take that one. The matches where I beat him were worth a lot more. Especially the first one.

Chapter 11

Poker Players As TV Stars

In his autobiography, prosaically titled *Moneymaker*, Chris Moneymaker tells the story of his first "WTF" moment as world champion.

After his night of steeply elevated blood-alcohol levels and excessive Vegas strip-club tabs, he stumbled into the airport for an early-morning flight, passed out on the plane, and pulled himself together for a "surprise" party (which he saw coming) organized for him by his wife, Kelly, at the Bound'ry, the restaurant where he worked. More than 200 people were there to celebrate Nashville's new millionaire—mostly friends and family, with a few less recognizable faces mixed in.

One of those faces belonged to a guy with whom Chris had played a round of golf a couple of weeks before. They weren't friends, by any means, but they certainly weren't strangers, having spent four or five hours sharing a cart on the links just before Moneymaker left for Vegas.

And here was this acquaintance suddenly calling him "Mr. Moneymaker" and asking him to pose for photos together and sign autographs for him.

Moneymaker had been poker champ of the world for less than 24 hours. And already, that world was changing. He wasn't just newly rich. He was newly famous. At least a little.

Before long, that little would turn into a lot.

Of all the scenarios that crossed Moneymaker's mind as

he packed his bags for Vegas when he was chasing a long-shot goal of maybe, just maybe, making the money and scoring a $15,000 min-cash, becoming famous wasn't one of them. No connection between fame and poker existed in the spring of 2003. Nor did the notions of poker players having publicists and agents or signing endorsement deals with online sites. Saying, "I'm going to become a poker star" in the spring of '03 would have been like saying, "I'm going to become a reality-TV star" the first time MTV cast for *The Real World*.

PokerStars existed before Moneymaker won the World Series. Poker stars did not.

Everyone who succeeded in the "poker industry" (another term that didn't really exist before '03) in the time period that immediately followed Moneymaker's win did so by thinking on their feet, improvising, reacting to the world changing around them, and selecting the right waves to ride. If you thought, *Online poker ain't real poker; I don't want anything to do with it*, or if you thought, *I don't want to play on TV, everyone will learn all my secrets*, then you got left behind and missed out on a whole lot of money that was about to be pumped into your game.

In 2003, the World Poker Tour was airing on Travel Channel and the WSOP was about to join it on ESPN. That was the extent of televised poker in America.

By 2006, if you typed "poker" into your TiVo search, you could fill about 50 hours a week with shows like "Poker Superstars," "Celebrity Poker Showdown," NBC's "National Heads-Up Poker Championship," "Poker After Dark," "High Stakes Poker," and countless other shows that came and went quickly (anyone remember "Hollywood Home Game" on E! or ABC's "Pro/Am Poker Equalizer"?). TV programmers couldn't get enough, and if you were one of the world's top 100 or 200 tournament-poker players, you were a celebrity.

Chapter 11 returns to several interview subjects we haven't heard from in a while, including brother-and-sister poker pros Howard Lederer and Annie Duke, ESPN play-by-play man Lon McEachern, and ESPN executives Bob Chesterman, Fred Christenson, and Mike Antinoro.

How could this chapter *not* include insights from the ESPN folks? The idea of poker players as TV stars wouldn't have been possible without the world's most visible sports network taking a gamble on poker in 2003.

"Get used to it. You're famous now."

Nolan Dalla: After my work was done at the Horseshoe on the night of the final table, I turned my cell phone off and went to bed.

When I woke up, my voice mail was full. Completely full.

How it worked was that if anybody called the Horseshoe about anything relating to the World Series or to publicity, it went straight to Nolan Dalla's cell phone. So I had literally about 60 messages on my phone. And I didn't know any of the numbers.

So I start dialing these things back, and it's area code 212 and 202—it's New York, Washington, Los Angeles. And I get to one, and I call this 212 number, and the voice on the other end answers, "David Letterman Show!"

That's when it hit me. I realized at that moment that poker had changed, the World Series had changed, my life had changed. And then Chris Moneymaker was on "Letterman" a couple weeks later.

Chris Moneymaker: My biggest fear in life was public speaking. And for them to tell me I was going on "David Letterman" or "Jimmy Kimmel" or any of these shows, I just told them straight up, "No, I'm not going to do it."

I had to do media junkets and interviews and all this stuff, and every time for the first six months, I felt like I had to throw up before I went on air. I really felt sick from the stress that I was under, trying to make it through the interviews.

Obviously, over time, they got easier. And when you do your biggest one first, it definitely makes the other ones easier. "Letterman" was my first interview, and I survived it, and then "Kimmel" after that. By the time I got to doing "The To-day Show" a couple years later, I was comfortable enough. But in '03, they had to push pretty damn hard to get me to do "Letterman."

Dalla: When Moneymaker came on "Letterman," I was in the poker room at the Horseshoe. We turned up the volume on the TVs and I remember watching Letterman complete-ly flub up the name of the casino. He didn't call it Binion's Horseshoe. He called it the Golden Horseshoe in downtown Las Vegas. And the Golden Nugget was one of our biggest competitors!

Dan Goldman: Part of our "contract" for the World Se-ries, when you won a seat, was you agreed to represent Pok-erStars. But it was very abstract and we didn't have the legal language that we should have. There was sort of an obliga-tion, but it wasn't really spelled out what that obligation was.

So we decided to be proactive and make a very aggres-sive proposal to Chris to represent us. The World Series end-ed on a Friday and Chris and I talked about it a couple of times that weekend.

I drove back from Las Vegas to L.A. the following Mon-day, which was Memorial Day, and Chris called me. I remem-ber exactly where I was when the phone rang—I was making my annual stop at Alien Fresh Jerky in Baker [California].

Chris tells me he's decided that he doesn't want the limelight and he's just going to take his money and go back to work. And, in fact, he was calling me *from work. On Memorial Day.* I thought that was a really bad sign for us.

Moneymaker: I went back to my job. I was back at work Monday morning. I didn't think of poker as a career option.

Goldman: I said, "Chris, all I can ask is that you think this over. You've got a one-time opportunity here to capitalize on winning the most prestigious poker tournament in the world and frankly, you've got a name that will play in an extraordinary way in the market. You just need to think it over. I would urge you to take a couple of days before you make a decision and consider how this is going to affect your future."

He agreed to do that.

I think he was overwhelmed by the money. He'd been struggling financially when he came out to the World Series; he'd sold significant chunks of himself to his father and a friend. And all of a sudden, this financial pressure is gone and a company is offering him significant additional money. It was a really difficult situation for him.

And there's nobody you can turn to. It's not like you can go hire a manager, because at the time, there were no people managing poker players. Who do you turn to for advice in a situation like that? So he needed some time.

We didn't talk for almost a week. The following Saturday or Sunday, he called me and said, "Okay, I see your point. I don't want to sign up to go on the road for a year, but I'm in. Let's see where this goes."

Mike Moneymaker: Chris quit his job. He said, "I can be an accountant when I'm 50."

Moneymaker: One of the big changes in my life was that I got divorced that year. The main reason was me wanting to be a traveling poker pro.

She didn't sign up for that life. I wasn't that person when we got married and she really didn't have the desire to be married to a poker player. She was married to a stay-at-home accountant who wasn't traveling the world, gone all the time, and gambling a lot of money.

It was a choice I had to make.

I tried to be good, stay at my job, and be that accountant, but in all honesty I didn't want to. I realized I could make money doing appearances. I was making money in cash games. That felt like something I wanted to pursue.

Mike Moneymaker: Other than the career change, the money really didn't change Chris. He's still down to earth, still very grounded. I haven't seen any negative changes.

David Gamble: If you get to know Chris, he's really just a down-to-earth quiet guy. Chris is not going to be the one that walks into a big room and starts shaking hands and talking to people, unless they start talking to him.

This should tell you the kind of person Chris is. For my percentage of the payout, we had a handshake deal. There was no contract or whatever. He turned around and wrote me a check for my 20% as soon as it was over.

My $2,000 investment, and whatever I spent on the room, and whatever I spent when we were out there, that turned out to be a really good investment when Chris wrote me the check.

Mike Moneymaker: My wife knew Chris won the seat and was going to Las Vegas, but she didn't know about the $2,000. She found that out after he won it.

I said, "What would you say to a return on investment of $2,000 coming back as $500,000?"

She said, "I'd say it's a Ponzi scheme."

I said, "Well, I don't know anybody named Ponzi, but that's what happened when Chris won."

She said, "Whaaaat?"

I said, "Yeah, we're gonna pay the house off first thing."

She said, "You got that right!"

Goldman: The World Series ended just before Memorial Day and the ESPN broadcast didn't start until July, so it really didn't have much of an impact for a couple months.

Chris came out to Los Angeles and shot some TV commercials with us before it started airing. I remember sitting on the rental-car shuttle bus going from LAX with him and asking, "Have things changed?"

He said, "You know, I've bought some stuff. I'm hearing from friends I haven't heard from in a while. But other than that, nothing's really changed."

Two weeks later, the ESPN broadcast happened and not long after that, we asked him to come out and play in the WPT Legends of Poker at the Bicycle Club. I picked him up at the airport. And he reminded me of that conversation we'd had the month before.

He said, "Yeah, things are a little different now. I walked off the plane and I got mobbed."

I said, "Well, get used to it. You're famous now."

Moneymaker: When the ESPN broadcasts first started airing, we had a big home poker game every Tuesday night. When it came on TV, the first time I saw myself, I turned to my friends and said, "Dude, am I really that fat?"

They said, "Yes, you are."

I'm like, "Well, fuck, I gotta go on a diet, because that's

embarrassing." I didn't realize how big I was.

That was my first reaction to seeing myself on TV. The camera's supposed to add 10 pounds. It added about 40 to me.

Annie Duke: I had a bunch of small kids then, so I was just in jeans and T-shirts. I was only going to play poker, so I didn't even think about making myself up. After seeing myself on television, I regretted that decision. By the time the Tournament of Champions rolled around, I had figured it out and had makeup on.

Matt Maranz: When we left Vegas, we all felt that it was a unique experience, like we had something that not many people had seen before. But we weren't sure how it was going to translate on television, because poker can be quite boring. It's nine people sitting at a table staring at each other.

After we edited the first hand, though, we came to the consensus that, *That's really compelling. We're not really sure why. But it's really compelling.*

Bob Chesterman: When this guy Moneymaker ends up winning it, we knew we kind of captured lightning in a bottle as far as programming and production. We knew we captured good content and a good show. But we didn't have any sort of idea it was going to blow up like it did.

Maranz: A TV show being good doesn't mean people are actually going to watch it. Then the first episode aired and the ratings were good. People were surprised.

Initially, ESPN was like, "That has to be a mistake. That's one of those ratings statistical blips."

So they put it on again and it did really well again.

They tried moving it around in different programming

spots, because I think in their mind, it just didn't compute to what a successful television show was supposed to be. They'd try at two in morning, four in the morning, 10 at night, and no matter where they re-aired it, it was getting big ratings.

So it was almost to the point of, "Where's the worst place we can put it?" And they put it there and it still did well.

Fred Christenson: The ratings, they were a notch below the NFL and college football, but there wasn't much else that it wasn't beating. They were doing over a 1, which was unheard of.

Maranz: No one saw this coming. No one saw how big it was going to be, and anyone who says they did is lying to you.

Mike Antinoro: I think most people at ESPN, with the exception of Will Staeger, were surprised. Will was convinced it was going to work. I don't even know if Fred thought it would work as well as it did. It was pretty different for ESPN.

With live events and news and information, you know if you have something that's going to rate. A lot of the ESPN Original Entertainment stuff we were trying was really strong programming, but there's a period there where you have to get the audience to accept something new, then hopefully word of mouth builds and people start to tune in week after week.

The World Series of Poker brought in college basketball game numbers right from the start. It was huge.

Right away, the people at ESPN got excited about it, as soon as the first numbers came in.

Then Shapiro put the full force of ESPN's promotional machine behind it—not just promotions on the air, but putting stuff on "SportsCenter." It became a focus of the network right away. We really capitalized on it.

Norman Chad: It was stunning to me. I had no idea, even if we put a great product on TV, that anyone would watch it. At the end of the day, it's a bunch of middle-aged men throwing chips into the middle of the table. It doesn't seem to be TV-friendly from that very narrow standpoint.

But when I first saw the product they put out, before we voiced it, I told Lon, "All me and you can do is screw this up. This is really good. They really know what they're doing!"

Then, watching the ratings, I couldn't believe that it was resonating this well with people.

Dave Swartz: We covered poker as a kind of documentary/sports hybrid with character development being a paramount piece of it, so it led to this thing where for seven straight weeks, people started watching it like it was reality television—along the lines of "Survivor" or "The Apprentice." And every week, it just started gaining this buzz. It came out with pretty strong ratings and it kept growing week after week.

Once you saw the ratings each week, and once *Entertainment Weekly* was writing about it as television's dirty little secret or whatever the quote was, you knew that it was really catching on.

Throughout those seven shows, ratings were building. Buzz was building.

Chad: I knew the ratings were just going to grow each week in those seven broadcasts. I knew that whatever good news we were getting at the beginning, it was going to get better.

Remember, this was before poker entered anything

close to the mainstream, so most people watching it had no idea who was going to win. It was plausibly live to them. So it was going to build the audience in a great way.

Several years earlier, ABC aired the show "Twin Peaks." I hated "Twin Peaks," but when I watched it, because of the way it was constructed, I told people, "If you don't watch this from the beginning, you have no idea what's going on. You cannot join 'Twin Peaks' in Episode Four." That show could only go down in the ratings every week; it wasn't going to build an audience.

Well, this was the opposite of "Twin Peaks." This was word of mouth going around: "You gotta watch these people. It's unbelievable."

Maranz: When it became clear it was a ratings hit, they just started airing it nonstop all the time on all the different ESPN networks.

Antinoro: We didn't want to "Who Wants To Be A Millionaire" it, but the ratings were too good not to re-air it a lot.

It's funny. We'd fight Shapiro with some of the EOE programming, because as much as he supported us philosophically, if he could get a higher rating with a re-air of "Baseball Tonight," he would do it. That's his job, to get a high rating. So we would have to fight for a re-air of our stuff.

But we didn't have to fight for poker. Wherever he could put it, he would put it.

Chesterman: The re-airs did unbelievably well. That's why you saw it so much; after airing number 25, it's still holding up with a decent rating. Our programming guys, they were able to schedule it here and there and fill lots of holes, and it was still making money on the re-airs.

McEachern: Anywhere I went, we looked up months and months afterward and we saw closeups of Sam Farha and Chris Moneymaker. They were running that show *forever*.

Chad: I had no idea it was going to be rebroadcast ad nauseum.

Poker, during the biggest part of the poker boom, was on ESPN more than anything else other than "SportsCenter." That was a stunning revelation. And it changed the way that I looked at doing the broadcasts, because when you do a live broadcast, it's there and it's gone two hours later. But these things are going to be re-aired 10 times, 20 times, 30 times. If you sound stupid or you talk too much or you make a mistake, it's exacerbated by the fact that it's going to re-air that many times. So it made me think twice about what I was saying. It made me think twice about talking too much.

Dan Harrington: Sometime that fall, I'm in Philadelphia. I exit a hotel and someone says, "Hey, Dan, how are you?"

I turn around and it's like, *Gee, I don't recognize this person at all.* So I decide, let me just act like I know him. "I'm fine, how are you?" And I figure maybe he'll give me a clue as to who he is, so I can finally connect it.

And he says, "You did great on TV." So, okay, I got TV recognition. That's a little bit unusual.

I walk down the street. There's some insurance product I want to know about, a financial product, so I walk in there. There's a clerk at the desk and I start to say, "Hey, my name is—"

And he says, "I know who you are, Mr. Harrington."

I was like, *Holy Christ, this thing is on TV, everyone knows who the hell I am, and I didn't even win the damn tournament! What's going on here?* That's when I started to realize what the impact was.

I asked an ESPN producer the next year, "Look, I understand the first four or five times you put the thing on TV, but the 120th time you put it on TV? What's that about?"

He looked at me and said, "It beat hockey."

Daniel Negreanu: That period of time was the most exciting period for poker in its history. Seeing poker on ESPN in prime time—not only that, the coverage was fantastic, everything was exciting about it, it was so new and fresh. Just feeling like, *Oh my gosh, this is ready to explode!*

Side Action

Nolan Dalla: I was in the office when, about two months after the World Series aired, we got an offer—I can't tell you who it was from; I just can't say that—but we got an offer to sell the World Series of Poker, to break it off from the Horseshoe and sell just the World Series name and rights for $4 million cash.

It was just an intellectual property. All you were buying was the name. And the casino was hemorrhaging money, so $4 million sounds pretty attractive.

But the offer was rejected. And then Harrah's ends up buying the Horseshoe and gets the World Series with it.

Fred Christenson: If I recall, the feds shut down Binion's—they literally put yellow tape around the building and shut it down. The casino was backed up on pension payments to the employees, and that's when Harrah's swooped in and bought it. I think that was in the fall of '03.

Howard Lederer: Management was having trouble maintaining the property and maintaining good standing with the regulator, so Harrah's bought the Horseshoe brand from Jack Binion, in like some $1.7 billion deal.

Harrah's didn't know what they bought when they bought Binion's. They were looking to flip the property and I remember hearing a few weeks after they had made that purchase that they were already sending out feelers for who might be interested in buying it. But they said that like 90% of their phone calls were from people inquiring as to whether they could buy the World Series from them. I think that's when it dawned on them, *Wait a second, I think we just bought something here.*

It's an interesting little piece of history. I honestly believe that Harrah's was not buying the World Series of Poker when they made that purchase. They were just buying the Horseshoe.

Christenson: I remember getting a call in the middle of the night that Harrah's was buying them. I got up first thing in the morning and faxed [Harrah's CEO] Gary Loveman the World Series of Poker contract with ESPN, like, "You have to honor this," because this was Year One. They inherited this contract.

Harrah's and Gary Loveman did everything in their power to get out from under it, because it was so one-sided. But they ultimately did honor the contract.

Chapter 12

The Boom Begins

On November 5, 2013, at a little past 9 p.m. Las Vegas time, tears began welling in Ryan Riess' eyes. He was one card away from being crowned the world champion of poker. Riess' A-K led Jay Farber's Q-5 when they got it all-in pre-flop, it led after the flop missed them both, and it led after the turn missed them both. When a harmless four fell on the river, the 23-year-old kid from Michigan collapsed to the floor on the stage at the Rio All-Suite Hotel & Casino's Penn & Teller Theatre, while family and friends descended from the bleachers to create the sort of pile-on normally seen on the pitcher's mound after the final out of baseball's World Series is recorded.

Riess had only been a poker pro for about year when he captured the championship bracelet and the $8.3 million payout attached to it. But he'd been playing poker for a decade.

"I've been dreaming about it for a long time," Riess said into the ESPN microphone, "ever since I was 14 and saw Moneymaker win it."

Children of the Moneymaker Effect have been taking over the poker world chip by chip since 2003. In fact, the ages of the six Main Event champions crowned from 2008-2013 have been 22, 21, 23, 22, 24, and 23. And nothing could have underscored the shift in poker's generational demographics more perfectly than Ryan Riess winning on the 10th anniversary of Moneymaker's historic triumph. Watching the then-27-year-old Moneymaker win on ESPN in '03 planted the poker bug inside Riess' brain and he soon started hosting twice-weekly $10 games in his basement. Fast-forward 10 years and he's a millionaire eight times over.

The so-called Moneymaker Effect, of course, went far beyond just infusing the game with young blood. It was really about infusing poker with new blood of all varieties—millions upon millions of people who were unaware or only casually aware of no-limit Texas hold 'em before ESPN first televised Moneymaker's triumph (then televised it again and again and again) and found themselves wanting to either start playing the game for fun or dreaming of following in Chris' seven-figure footsteps. Then there were those who didn't watch Moneymaker win, but got invited to the home game of a buddy who did and, indirectly, got hooked on poker via the Moneymaker Effect. The numbers grew, and grew, and grew, and before long, poker was *everywhere*.

The point of contention that still remains is to what extent poker boomed because of Moneymaker's win and to what extent it boomed because it was ready to boom in 2003 no matter what, with ESPN and the Internet converging on the game.

That's a discussion nearly everyone interviewed for this oral history weighs in on in Chapter 12, including:
- poker pros Kenna James, Howard Lederer, Erik Seidel, Phil Hellmuth, Cory Zeidman, Daniel Negreanu, Barry Greenstein, Phil Ivey, Sam Farha, Annie Duke, Jeff Shulman, and Greg Raymer;
- hole-card-camera inventor Henry Orenstein;
- *Rounders* co-writer Brian Koppelman;
- Binion's Horseshoe Director of Public Relations Nolan Dalla;

- poker journalists John Vorhaus and Peter Alson;
- ESPN Original Entertainment Senior Coordinating Producer Bob Chesterman;
- ESPN play-by-play man Lon McEachern;
- 441 Productions Executive Producer Matt Maranz;
- Vegas handicapper Lou Diamond;
- and WSOP Tournament Director Matt Savage.

Just how much did Chris Moneymaker change poker? The answer to that question will long be debated. But there's no debate about it in Ryan Riess' household.

> *"Anyone who says they could have predicted the extent to which poker exploded, they're lying."*

Kenna James: When it's going on and you're in it, it's really hard to say how big it's going to be. It's like people in the music business, when they record a song that later becomes a mega-hit. "Did you know this was going to be a mega-hit?" And the truth is you don't really know, but you sense something is afoot.

Howard Lederer: Erik Seidel called me the day after Moneymaker won. He said, "Can you believe that Moneymaker won?" Erik got it right away, that it was going to change everything. He said, "This is the best thing that could happen to poker."

Erik Seidel: This is a well-known story: As the final table was being played, [poker pro] Mike Matusow was at the

Horseshoe saying, "If this guy wins the tournament, I'm gonna kill myself. It's the worst thing ever for poker." He was going through one of his Mikey rants.

I said, "Are you kidding me? If he wins, we should give 5% of all our future earnings to him. Because to have an amateur with this name and this story win is gonna change poker."

To me, it was immediately apparent. You knew his story. He got in for $40, he was a rank amateur, he had this incredible name, and he was running over people. It just looked like if this guy can do it, everyone's going to think they can do it.

Brian Koppelman: Chris Moneymaker—the name, the story, the way he won. Chris was an accountant who won an online tournament to gain entry and turned that into $2.5 million. It's the exact fantasy.

It would be like if your local teaching pro won the PGA Championship, imagine what would happen to golf in America. In poker, there's one major, and the equivalent of the local hacker got in there and won the thing. Suddenly, everybody was able to justify playing poker. You're telling your wife you're going to the World Series of Poker and it wasn't a crazy thing. It was a good investment.

Phil Hellmuth: I remember thinking that if Moneymaker wins, it's just gotta be huge for poker. Poker was already about to take off and now you have an amateur, an accountant from Tennessee, with a name like that, winning. You can see him doing "Letterman," you can see him doing "Leno."

I was also the guy who told a couple of famous writers in '97 that eventually poker would be played in a small stadium. I was the one who thought poker would become a huge sport on television. I was the one who saw the wave coming and told everybody. Everybody used to laugh at me back then. But even I never thought it would get *this* big.

Lederer: I wrote a four-piece blog at the time about my four days in the Main Event and broke it down, and at the end of my piece, I said, "Well, maybe we'll get 1,100 entrants next year." Like I'd made some outrageous prediction that we might jump from 839 to 1,100. I thought that was a pretty daring prediction.

Of course, it surpassed 2,500. It tripled in one year.

Lon McEachern: It had been such a slow glacial growth of the Main Event field that the pros who'd been doing it for years couldn't envision what was going to happen. *Yeah, it's gonna be good; yeah, we're gonna have more people next year, another 200 people; move it past 1,000, that would be cool.*

Henry Orenstein: When the whole thing started, there were 500 poker rooms in this country. Now there are 5,000.

Dalla: There were probably about 20 legitimate journalists credentialed for the World Series in '03, and about 150 in 2004.

John Vorhaus: Imagine the poker-book section of your local bookstore. In 2002, that section was half a shelf. By 2004, it was a floor-to-ceiling rack.

Peter Alson: Anyone who says they could have predicted the extent to which poker exploded, they're lying.

I think anybody you ask who answers that question with a modicum of honesty will say that they were blown away. We just never expected that kind of explosion.

It really was a perfect storm. It was the perfect storm of the Internet and Moneymaker and television, those three things combined. And I don't think you can actually say that one of those things had more of an impact than another. I really think it was the combination of all three.

Vorhaus: I have what I call the "poker-porn theory." When you're watching pornography, it doesn't make you want to do anything so much as it makes you want to do the thing you see on the screen. Well, when you're watching poker, it doesn't make you want to do anything so much as the thing you're watching unfold on the screen.

The manifestation of online poker suddenly meant that anybody who had that urge to scratch the itch, to mix metaphors, suddenly could scratch the itch. You watch it on TV and you can go satisfy your urge with online poker.

James: There's got to be fuel in the tank of a car for it to move. You had the lipstick cameras, the WPT, and everything. But Chris Moneymaker, he was poker's fuel that made it run.

Cory Zeidman: Poker was going to boom that year no matter who won the Main Event. If it was a pro, maybe it would have been slightly slower. But it was going to boom with or without Moneymaker. I feel 100% sure of that.

Bob Chesterman: I think Moneymaker is critical to getting it out there to the masses. There are people who wouldn't be watching poker right now if it wasn't for him. He was able to bring it to the casuals.

But I also think the World Series of Poker itself would have exploded without him. Nobody knows how big it would have exploded, but I do think it was ripe.

Negreanu: The wheels were in motion, we just needed

some kind of explosion. And it was like the perfect storm, really. A guy named Chris Moneymaker put $40 on a website and turned it into $2.5 million. It was the perfect story for the everyman.

If it had been someone other than Moneymaker, I don't think it would have been three times as big the next year. Maybe it would have doubled, but not tripled.

Barry Greenstein: You had all these online sites advertising on all these shows, that's what fueled it.

People like to say Chris Moneymaker winning was the perfect storm, but realistically, his winning was far less relevant than the hole-card camera and online poker. People had won on a satellite entry before; it just wasn't an online satellite and it didn't happen at the right time. That year, 2003, was the right time. Poker was primed to take off. Poker was already taking off.

Matt Maranz: The right guy won. The amateur who was poker's aspirational programming. You watch it, then you go, "Hey, that accountant from Tennessee, he's not that different from me. I could do that too." If a pro wins, you might not get that same boom effect.

Phil Ivey: It made everybody feel that they had a chance to win, once he won. An amateur player came there and beat a professional, Sammy Farha, on the biggest stage in the world in poker. And he outplayed him a couple hands—which happens, anybody can outplay anyone in poker—and it made people feel like they had a chance to do it. It was one of the best things that could ever happen in poker.

Hellmuth: Moneymaker was great for everybody. And I think that he's a great representative of the game.

Sammy Farha: I don't think Moneymaker winning made any difference. Even if I won, it would have been the same result. Poker was going to boom in 2003 no matter who won. Moneymaker helped it, but it didn't matter if he came first, second, or third. It didn't make a difference if he won $2.5 million or $1.3 million—that's a lot of money either way. Forty bucks got you a million dollars? It's beautiful.

Actually, poker would have been more booming if Sammy would have won it, because Sammy would have had more money in his pocket and gambling would be better.

Vorhaus: Moneymaker was the cherry on the sundae. And the "Moneymaker Effect" is such a great shorthand for what was going on in poker at the time. It wouldn't have worked as well if it was called "The Farha Effect."

Alson: I often fantasized about what would have happened if there had just been Moneymaker and television, but no Internet, because for people like me who came up playing live cash games and tournaments, the golden age of poker of there being a lot of bad players to play against would have lasted a lot longer.

In the old days, the learning curve was long, torturous, and expensive. So it just seemed so unfair to players like me who came up the old way that these kids could learn on the Internet, starting for little money, and be able to learn exponentially faster. What took me 15 or 20 years, they could learn in a matter of months.

Lederer: There are great live players who can't play online, and there are great online players who can't play live, but some of these online players turn into great live players. So we knew that there were going to be some of these online players that were going to translate well to the live game and were going to change the game.

Farha: Poker changed a lot from 2003 to these days. Now there's a lot of great players, and there's a lot of fearless players. I used to be the only Sammy Farha before 2003. Now they're all Sammy Farhas.

Annie Duke: It was at a $5,000 WPT event at Borgata in the fall of 2003 that I first really understood what had happened. There were like 500 players or something and that was just unheard of outside the World Series Main Event. If you played a $5,000 preliminary event at the World Series of Poker prior to 2003, you were talking about 50 to 100 players. Now all of a sudden, I go to Borgata and it's like 500 players or something.

Then I sat down at a table and watched a hand where a player raised, and then another player re-raised, and then the first player moved all-in for a good amount of chips, and the other guy called and couldn't get his money in fast enough … and he flips over A-3 offsuit like it's just the frickin' nuts.

So that was a big moment for me, where I realized how bad the fish were now.

Moneymaker: When I played the WPT, I didn't know what the field size was supposed to be. The first WPT event I played was a little smaller than 839, so that seemed normal. I didn't know that back in the day, there were like 30 people playing in these big tournaments. In my limited life in poker, all these tournaments had tons of people.

So it wasn't until the 2004 World Series, when I got out there and you couldn't even walk in the Horseshoe and the sit-and-go lines were hours upon hours long, that I realized the game had gotten a lot more popular. I didn't realize the full impact on poker until that next year, when I went out there and I saw all the crazies.

Jeff Shulman: One of my jokes was, I'd tell all these pros, "Someday there are going to be little hotties following poker." And everyone's like, "Yeah, right." If you were in poker pre-2003, you understood that it was just a bunch of old dudes and their wives. But I was like, "At some point, we're going to get some younger people in and maybe there's going to be some hotties that watch poker kinda like sports," and then within two or three years, there were spectators and it all came true. The poker demographic became much younger, which you can't deny has something to do with Moneymaker.

Duke: People weren't putting on a show for the cameras yet in 2003, because they didn't realize that they could be marketing themselves. After that boom, there were people who came to play poker specifically to get on television.

Matt Savage: At the 2004 World Series, we definitely were not anticipating 2,576 players. We actually ran out of chips! One night we had to open the bags up and replace some of the chips with smaller denominations, so that we could run the next day. That was an all-night affair.

We also almost got shut down by the fire department.

We had 11-handed tables at the start of the tournament, which I hated, obviously, but we did whatever we could to get everybody in the tournament.

This was after splitting it into two Day Ones, a decision I made that some people fought against. Some people said, "No, we don't need that, we can do alternates," not expecting how big the field would get. As we got closer, the folks at Binion's realized we were going to have a lot more players than the year before and they agreed to have two Day Ones.

Greg Raymer: I was extremely surprised by the turnout the year I won. Matt Savage was relatively prepared for this huge burst and that's why he made two Day Ones, and still he didn't have anywhere near enough space.

My starting table was a stud table, only meant to seat eight players. So we were very uncomfortable. Then all of a sudden, this guy comes walking up with chips and a rack and he says, "Excuse me, I'm your 11-seat."

It turns out they had a handful of tables in one of the aisles at the front of the casino, and the fire marshal came by and said, "You have 10 minutes to clear this aisle or I'm going to shut down the whole building."

So Matt did the only thing he could, which was to make these people the 11-seat at various tables. It's a crap solution, but every option is horrible. It's like, which horrible option is Matt going to pick?

The numbers were just so much more than anyone ever expected. If Matt hadn't done two Day Ones, they would have had to turn half the field away. I might have flown all the way there and not been able to play.

The butterfly effect, every little thing mattered, or I might not have won.

Negreanu: The seams were about to burst on the Horseshoe. The Horseshoe had always been a place where you had a couple hundred people; it was very comfortable. Then all of a sudden in 2004, it was like, *Whoa, this place is going to explode.* There was just no room for it. It was getting too big for its own britches.

Lou Diamond: ESPN brought me back the next year. I

was probably the highest-paid P.A. ever.

These people are coming up to me, "Who do you like this year?" I picked Marcel Luske. And Marcel actually came in 10th out of 2,500 players!

Late in the tournament, Matt comes up to me and says, "Lou, if Marcel wins this, I think we're going to have to do a story on you." Then, *bam*, 20 minutes later Marcel gets booted in 10th place.

Moneymaker: A lot of people came up to me the next few years and said, "You're responsible for this." Or, "Thanks a lot; I can't get on a table now."

I obviously had an idea that I was a big catalyst for it, but can I really say I caused this?

I don't think in those terms. I never thought in those terms. I'm just a guy who got a little lucky and played really good poker for one week. And I picked the best week in history to do that.

Epilogue

It has been more than 10 years since Chris Moneymaker's magical run birthed the poker boom and set into motion an insanely eventful decade for the game. Live-tournament numbers grew exponentially. Every major TV network, and most of the minor ones, launched poker programming. The Commerce and the Bicycle casinos replaced the Viper Room nightclub as the hottest celebrity hangouts in Hollywood. Online poker became a mammoth international industry, where Sunday tournaments generated eight-figure prize pools and nosebleed-stakes cash games routinely produced individual pots in the high six figures.

But the news wasn't all sunshine and gumdrops. Measurements of the health of poker post-2003 are directly connected to the online game, which is directly connected to what the United States government decides is its role in decreeing how citizens can spend their time and money. In 2006, members of Congress attached the Unlawful Internet Gambling Enforcement Act to an unrelated port-security bill and suddenly, the legality of collecting and dispersing money for online poker became unclear, scaring many sites out of the U.S. market. Those that remained, such as PokerStars, Full Tilt Poker, and UltimateBet/AbsolutePoker, prospered. Until April 15, 2011, that is. On the date poker players know as "Black Friday," the Department of Justice indicted the operators of those sites and blocked American players from using them.

The live-tournament numbers suggest that interest in poker hasn't necessarily waned; only access to online games has. And that access is coming back: In 2013, online poker began achieving legalization and regulation on a state-by-state basis, with Nevada, New Jersey, and Delaware leading the charge. If and when more states follow, a second poker boom looms. The game is changing again.

Certainly, the lives of most of those interviewed for this 2003 WSOP history have changed considerably over the past decade-plus. Here's an update on everyone quoted in the book, in the order in which they appeared.

Chris Moneymaker

Following his divorce from wife Kelly, Chris re-married and he and second wife Christy and their three children now live in Memphis. He remains a touring poker pro with a PokerStars sponsorship deal that helps provide stability in the face of the financial swings of playing poker for a living.

In March 2004, Moneymaker finished second in a WPT event for $200,000, and he bettered that in 2011 with a second-place finish in NBC's National Heads-Up Poker Championship for $300,000. He hasn't managed to cash in the WSOP Main Event again in 10 tries after '03, but his lifetime tournament earnings are now more than $3.5 million and he's generally regarded as a solid pro, if not one of the game's absolute elite.

Brian Koppelman

Along with writing partner David Levien, Koppelman has continued to expand his IMDB page, most famously as writers of the *Ocean's Eleven* sequel *Ocean's Thirteen*. They've continued operating in the poker-fiction space as well, with the 2005 ESPN TV series "Tilt" and the 2013 movie *Runner Runner*, set in the world of online gaming.

Brian also dabbled in acting, became a contributor to Grantland.com, and, with Levien, directed the ESPN "30 For 30" documentary "This Is What They Want" about tennis great Jimmy Connors. Additionally, a sequel to *Rounders* is potentially in the offing.

Koppelman played online at Full Tilt Poker as a sponsored "Friend of Full Tilt," until Black Friday intervened.

Daniel Negreanu

"Kid Poker" has ascended to stardom as comprehensively as anyone in the game, with his remarkable run book-ended by Poker Player of the Year recognition in both 2004 and 2013. He ranks third on the all-time tournament money list with more than $19 million in cashes, has won four more WSOP bracelets (bringing his career total to six), has captured two WPT titles, and is the face of PokerStars.

He has married, divorced, and gone vegan, plus he writes blogs and film vlogs, launched a poker training site, wrote a strategy book, and co-starred in a reality show.

Henry Orenstein

Now in his 90s, the odds-defying Orenstein is still going strong, playing in cash games in Atlantic City every weekend and traveling yearly to the WSOP. He brought the "Poker Superstars Invitational" to Fox SportsNet as creator and executive producer and he was one of the producers of the enormously popular "High Stakes Poker." He was invited to play in the inaugural NBC National Heads-Up Poker Championship in '05 and won his first-round match before falling in round two.

Henry was inducted into the Poker Hall of Fame in 2008.

Cory Zeidman

Florida-based part-time pro and seven-card-stud specialist Zeidman won his first WSOP bracelet in a stud hi-lo event in 2012, but he's better known for a single no-limit hold 'em hand: In 2005, Cory rivered a straight flush to beat Jennifer Harman's full house at the TV table on Day One of the WSOP Main Event, a hand that has been replayed and discussed perhaps as much as any since Moneymaker's bluff.

Zeidman has been a (highly opinionated) columnist for *ALL IN* magazine since 2006.

John Vorhaus

Vorhaus has written an estimated two million words in the past 10 years, some of them about poker—most notably, the 2011 strategy book he co-authored with Annie Duke, *Decide to Play Great Poker*. He has also written six novels (two of them about poker) and has taught writing courses in 30 countries on five continents.

Additionally, John reached the final table of the WSOP's seniors (age 50 and over) event in 2006, finishing ninth.

Jeff Shulman

The Shulman family still runs *CardPlayer* magazine, with Jeff acting as president and COO of CardPlayer Media.

Shulman has made five WSOP final tables since 2003, most notably at the 2009 Main Event, where he was part of the November Nine and finished fifth for more than $1.95

million. In total, Shulman boasts live-tournament earnings of more than $3.4 million.

Mike Sexton

The World Poker Tour is now in its 12th season (after a fair bit of network hopping) and Sexton remains its venerable on-air analyst, along with Vince Van Patten.

He's done his share on the felt as well: He won a cool $1 million for taking first place in the WSOP's Tournament of Champions in 2006, made WPT final tables in both 2011 and '13, and boasts career tournament earnings of more than $5.6 million. He also became a father for the first time in 2008, at the age of 60.

Sexton was inducted into the Poker Hall of Fame in 2009.

Dan Harrington

Harrington pulled off arguably the greatest multi-year feat in WSOP Main Event history in 2004, when he reached the final table again, finishing fourth just one year after placing third. He won the WPT's Legends of Poker Main Event in '07, making him one of only five WSOP Main Event champions to capture a WPT title, but he has slowed down his poker-playing schedule significantly in recent years.

Where he hasn't slowed down much is in the publishing game, as he wrote six poker-strategy books between 2004 and 2010.

Dan was inducted into the Poker Hall of Fame in 2010.

Kenna James

James was one of the steadiest earners on the tournament scene for three years after the 2003 World Series, cranking out seven separate six-figure scores, including a 44th place run in the '05 Main Event and a second-place finish at the '05 WPT Legends of Poker.

Kenna's success tapered off the next few years, however, and in '09, he reduced his poker schedule significantly and became a life coach.

At the height of the poker boom, he served as the on-air co-host of the syndicated program "Ultimate Poker Challenge," which lasted three seasons.

Nolan Dalla

Though the Horseshoe and the WSOP changed ownership in the months after Moneymaker's win, Dalla has remained on board throughout the decade-plus since as the director of public relations for the World Series.

Along with Peter Alson, he co-authored the biography *One of a Kind: The Rise and Fall of Stuey "The Kid" Ungar, the World's Greatest Poker Player*, and he blogs regularly at nolandalla.com.

Annie Duke

Duke emerged in the early years of the boom as the biggest female star in poker, winning a WSOP bracelet in '04, taking down the made-for-TV Tournament of Champions that same year, and capturing the NBC National Heads-Up Championship in 2010, while also coaching actor Ben Affleck to the California State Poker Championship and finishing as runner-up to Joan Rivers on "Celebrity Apprentice."

She wrote an autobiography and two poker strategy books, one with John Vorhaus, and has spearheaded numerous charitable enterprises, most notably the WSOP-affiliated Ante Up for Africa tournament.

However, she gained notoriety in 2012 when the poker league she co-founded with former WSOP Commissioner Jeffrey Pollack, the Epic Poker League, went bankrupt after only three events.

Greg Raymer

"Fossilman" was an unknown when he exited early from the 2003 Main Event, but as you surely know already if you've made it this far in the book, he became very much a known commodity the next year, when he won the WSOP Main Event and a $5 million first-place prize. Remarkably, in defense of his title the following year, Raymer finished 25th (and might have gone much deeper if not for a brutal beat), good for a payday of more than $300,000. In 2012, he won four Heartland Poker Tour events, and he's pushed his career live tournament earnings past $7.4 million.

He was sponsored by PokerStars from 2004-2011 and has been very active in the fight for online-poker regulation as a member of the Board of Directors of the Poker Players Alliance.

Greg was one of poker's most respected and beloved ambassadors until 2013, when he was arrested and charged with soliciting prostitution in North Carolina, but he is steadily working to rebuild his reputation.

Howard Lederer

Lederer went from one of poker's most successful and admired ambassadors to probably the game's most controversial figure after Black Friday. He was a founder and the president of Tiltware LLC, the parent company of Full Tilt Poker, which ascended to the peak of the online gaming world until indictments were handed down in 2011, at which time Full Tilt was unable to pay out its players and Howard and others were accused of misappropriating the company's funds. Lederer settled with the Department on Justice in 2012 for a reported $2.5 million, but he has been slow to return to visibility in the poker world.

All that said, he continued to excel on the tournament-poker scene between 2003 and 2011, mostly as a part-time player, racking up 10 six-figure cashes and one seven-figure score since the '03 World Series.

Sammy Farha

Farha remains more of a cash-game player than a tournament pro and has played his share of memorable hands in the cash-game show "High Stakes Poker," but he's also managed some noteworthy tournament achievements since his heads-up loss to Moneymaker. He won Omaha Hi-Lo WSOP bracelets in both 2006 and 2010 and has pushed his total tournament winnings to nearly $2.9 million.

He also penned the strategy book *Farha on Omaha* with ghostwriter Storms Reback.

Matt Savage

In 2003, Savage received the Benny Binion Award for outstanding service in the poker industry. Matt remained WSOP tournament director in 2004, but has since moved over to the World Poker Tour, where he serves as executive tour director and an on-air sideline reporter. He is also the tournament director at Commerce Casino in Los Angeles and at Bay 101 in his hometown of San José.

Matt currently lives in Las Vegas with his wife and two children.

Lon McEachern

McEachern has remained the play-by-play voice of ESPN poker straight through to the present; he gave up his job as a loan officer in 2005 when the network's poker coverage expanded beyond the point where he could make time for both careers.

Among Lon's other noteworthy credits are hosting the first network-TV mixed-martial-arts series, "Strikeforce on NBC," in 2009 and calling the action for ESPN's coverage of the 2012-'13 PBA Bowling Tour.

Barry Greenstein

Long a cash-game specialist, Greenstein earned the nickname the "Robin Hood of Poker" by giving all of his tournament winnings to charity in the early years of the poker boom. And those winnings were significant, as he claimed a WPT title and a WSOP bracelet in '04, another bracelet in '05, another WPT title in '06, and a third bracelet in '08. Barry's total live earnings now exceed $8 million.

In 2005, he wrote the popular book *Ace on the River*, and in 2011, Greenstein was inducted into the Poker Hall of Fame.

Mike Antinoro

After a couple more years with ESPN Original Entertainment (where they attempted unsuccessfully to do with darts what they'd done with poker), Antinoro left along with several other ESPN executives—including Mark Shapiro, Bob Chesterman, and Fred Christenson—to run marketing and communications and group sales at Six Flags, Inc.

In 2010, Antinoro became executive vice president of programming at Dick Clark Productions. Among his projects there, Mike is the executive producer of "Jim Rome on Show-time," which has reunited him with the production team of Matt Maranz and Dave Swartz from 441. Antinoro says he, Maranz, and Swartz frequently discuss getting back into poker programming, if they can find the right opportunity.

Bob Chesterman

Chesterman continued to serve as executive producer of the World Series of Poker coverage for the next four years (while working on numerous other ESPN projects as well) before leaving along with Shapiro, Antinoro, and Christenson to go to Six Flags, Inc. as vice president of park strategy and management.

In 2010, Bob left to become senior vice president of programming and production for the National Hockey League, where he is currently working on developing hockey's version of the hole-card cam, a small camera that can be built into a referee's helmet.

Fred Christenson

After nearly 20 years at ESPN, Christenson left in 2006 as part of the ESPN exodus to Six Flags, Inc., where he was regional vice president. In 2010, he became programming director at Dick Clark Productions.

A couple of years later, Fred started his own production company, Glen Oliver Company, which developed the show "Shark Hunters" for NBC SportsNet.

Christenson has also played quite a bit of poker over the years, both live and online, and cashed in a minor World Series event in 2007.

Matt Maranz

Maranz and 441 Productions continued to produce the World Series of Poker for ESPN until 2010, working on a total of more than 225 episodes across eight seasons. The company has produced numerous other poker programs, including the North American Poker Tour for ESPN, PokerStars Caribbean Adventure for GSN, and "Calvin Ayre's Wild Card Poker" for Fox SportsNet.

441 Productions has also created/produced such shows as "Jim Rome on Showtime" and VH1's "Heavy: The Story of Metal," and as of the end of 2013, they were working on a series on youth football called "Friday Night Tykes" and a Travel Channel series titled "Ace the Game."

Dave Swartz

Swartz continues to work for 441 Productions and has been promoted since 2003 from coordinating producer to executive producer. For a look at 441's credits post-2003, see the update on Matt Maranz above.

Erik Seidel

A long way removed from his days of being best known for losing the *Rounders*-replayed hand to Johnny Chan, Seidel is now fourth on the all-time tournament money list with more than $19 million and sixth on the all-time WSOP bracelet list with eight. He won bracelets in '05 and '07, won the NBC National Heads-Up Poker Championship in '11, claimed a WPT title in '08, and has significantly padded his bankroll with two seven-figure wins in super-high-roller events. Erik was a sponsored Full Tilt pro until Black Friday in 2011.

He was inducted into the Poker Hall of Fame in 2010.

Phil Hellmuth

Nobody took better advantage of the poker boom with self-marketing and branding than the "Poker Brat," who built a mini-industry out of his tableside tirades and choreographed late entrances. He's also added four WSOP bracelets to bring his career total to an unmatched 13 and won the inaugural NBC National Heads-Up Poker Championship in '05. In 2013, he scored his record 100th World Series cash.

Additionally, Hellmuth has written four books, released instructional DVDs, done TV commentary, attached his name to a mobile-phone game, and commanded up to $50,000 for public-speaking engagements.

Phil was inducted into the Poker Hall of Fame in 2007.

Norman Chad

Chad remains the wise-cracking voice of ESPN poker more than a decade after the network took a chance on him, still amusing audiences in tandem with straight-man Lon McEachern. He is also still writing his syndicated weekly "Couch Slouch" sports column and playing live mixed games whenever time allows.

Norman has cashed three times in World Series of Poker events, including a run to the final table of the $2,500 Omaha/stud hi-lo event in 2012.

Mike Moneymaker

After his son won the World Series, Mike used his 20% share to pay off his house in the Knoxville, Tennessee, area, but didn't experience a significant change of lifestyle. He continued working for the University of Tennessee, though he was forced to work from home in recent years due to health issues.

Sadly, while awaiting a lung transplant, Moneymaker passed away in March 2014, just prior to the publication of this book. Until his death, Mike remained very close with Chris.

Dan Goldman

Goldman remained the VP of marketing for PokerStars until 2007, when he ventured off in other online-gaming-related directions—as vice president of marketing for Duplicate Poker for a year, then as president and CEO of subscription online poker startup Fleet Street Games for three years, and now as executive vice president of Internet gaming for VCAT LLC.

He also blogs at smalltalkdan.com, where in 2013 he wrote a series of posts looking back on the '03 WSOP.

David Gamble

The year 2003 was big for Gamble and not just because he netted $300,000 or so post-tax from Moneymaker's WSOP win. Mere days later, he sold his health-care company for a considerably larger sum. He used some of the money to buy thoroughbred horses and to invest in musical artists as one half of Stampley Gamble Music based in "Music City U.S.A.," Nashville.

David and Chris remain friends, though they've seen each other only sparingly in recent years, since Moneymaker moved to Memphis.

Lou Diamond

Diamond remained a production assistant for ESPN at the World Series for five years.

He is still a sports handicapper in Vegas, selling his picks via his website louiediamond.com. And he stands by every word he was quoted saying in the WSOP oral history, even if other people's memories don't entirely align with his.

Peter Alson

Alson has published two high-profile poker books since the boom began, 2006's *One of a Kind: The Rise and Fall of Stuey "The Kid" Ungar, The World's Greatest Poker Player*, which he co-wrote with Nolan Dalla, and 2007's *Take Me to the River: A Wayward and Perilous Journey to the World Series of Poker*. He also ghost-wrote boxing trainer/broadcaster Teddy Atlas's autobiography *Atlas: From the Streets to the Ring, a Son's Struggle to Become a Man* and he works as a freelance writer and editor.

Dutch Boyd

Boyd claimed to have the highest fame-to-accomplishment ratio in poker—until 2006, when he won his first WSOP bracelet and the accomplishment began to catch up with the fame. In 2010, Dutch won a second bracelet, and in 2013, on the 10th anniversary of his '03 run, he cashed in the Main Event (as he'd also done in 2005). His total career live earnings now exceed $2.1 million.

Boyd has openly discussed his struggles with bipolar disorder and is currently working on a half-biography half-strategy book called *Poker Tilt*.

Phil Ivey

All the expectations surrounding Ivey as a poker player were met and exceeded over the next decade. As early as 2005, he was almost unanimously considered the best all-around player in the world, an unofficial title he's held onto consistently since then.

He's added five WSOP bracelets to bring his career total to nine, won a WPT title, run his career tournament earnings past $17 million, reached a Main Event final table (finishing seventh in '09), and succeeded in the biggest live and online cash games in existence.

He was sponsored by Full Tilt Poker from its launch through Black Friday, and now represents his own online brand, Ivey Poker.

Humberto Brenes

Brenes has remained a prominent presence on the poker tour, with two WPT final tables and five WSOP final tables since '03, plus an impressive four Main Event cashes in 10 years.

He also developed one of the least popular gimmicks of the TV-poker age, calling himself "the Shark" and bringing a toy shark to the table as a prop that developed into something resembling a ventriloquist's dummy. Thankfully, Brenes has toned that down in recent years, as he's grown into an elder statesman's role and poker ambassador, especially for the Latin American poker community.

Glossary of Poker Terms

all-in dark: putting all of your chips at risk without even looking at your cards

blinded off: when a player loses chips by not being seated at the table during a tournament

blinds: forced bets that two players have to pay on each hand (a "small blind" and a "big blind") to initiate action

bluff: a bet made with a mediocre or downright weak hand, designed to make a better hand fold

brick: fail to catch a card that improves your hand

c-bet: short for "continuation-bet," when the pre-flop raiser bets on the flop regardless of whether the community cards helped him

cooler: an unlucky situation in which a player has a strong hand, but another player has an even stronger one

counterfeit: when a turn or river card spoils a player's made hand; for example, with hole cards of 3-3, on a K-8-8-2 board, a king on the river would counterfeit the hand, because the player no longer holds a pair of threes, but rather holds kings and eights with a three kicker

covered: when one player has more chips going into the hand than the other player and can't be eliminated if he goes all-in

donkey: a derogatory term for a bad poker player

double up: to win an all-in hand against a larger stack and end up possessing twice as many chips as you started the hand with

dummy end: the low end of a straight, when a higher straight is possible

flat: call, as opposed to raise; short for "flat-call"

flip: short for "coin flip," a situation where two opposing hands are each about 50% likely to end up the best hand

four-bet: the fourth bet (also the third raise) in a given round of betting; pre-flop, if a player open-raises, then there's a re-raise, the next re-raise is a four-bet

freeroll: a tournament that costs nothing to enter

grinder: a player who puts in long hours in lower-stakes games

gutshot: a straight draw for which a single specific rank of card is required to complete the straight

hole cards: cards dealt face down to a player that can be used in that player's hand, but not in anyone else's

limp: in pre-flop action, to call the amount of the big blind, rather than folding or raising

money bubble: in a tournament, the point at which the next player eliminated won't make any money, but all of the other players remaining will

MTT: acronym for "multi-table tournament," a tournament that begins at a specific time and doesn't have a pre-set number of entries

muck: another term for fold

nuts: the best possible hand at that particular stage of the hand

open-ended: a straight draw in which the player already has four consecutive cards and can catch either the next lowest or next highest card to complete the straight

outs: board cards that will turn the inferior hand into the superior hand; the chances of an inferior hand improving are often measured by the number of "outs" the player has

overcard: either a hole card higher in rank than any board card, or a board card higher in rank than a player's pocket pair

overpair: a pocket pair that is higher in rank than any board card

PLO: acronym for pot-limit Omaha, a game that is similar to hold 'em, but in which each player is dealt four hole cards and must use exactly two of them

quads: another term for four-of-a-kind

rag: a small card, usually a six or below

rake: the amount of money taken by the house; in a cash game, it's a small amount taken from each pot, whereas in a tournament, it's a fee added to each player's buy-in before the tournament begins

satellite: a tournament in which winners qualify for another tournament with a larger buy-in

semi-bluff: a bet or raise made with a drawing hand that allows the bettor to win either by making the opponent fold or by catching a card later and making the best hand

set: three-of-a-kind made by combining paired hole cards with a matching community card

ship: another way of saying go all-in

sit-and-go: a tournament with a preset number of players that begins as soon as all the seats are filled

small ball: a style of play based around keeping pots moderately sized

suck out: hit a card that turns the inferior hand into the winning hand

tell: a physical or verbal mannerism that can reveal information about the strength of the player's hand

three-bet: the third bet (also the second raise) in a given round of betting; pre-flop, if a player open-raises, the first re-raise is a three-bet

under the gun: the first player to act in a betting round; usually refers to pre-flop position and the player to the immediate left of the big blind

The Rules of
No-Limit Texas Hold 'Em

Much of the hand description and strategy discussed on the preceding pages could cause confusion if you don't understand the rules of no-limit Texas hold 'em. So here's a quick primer.

The goal is to win pots either by making all other players fold their hands or by making the best five-card poker hand. The ranking of hands is as follows:

1. Straight flush (five cards in sequential order, all of the same suit; the best possible straight flush, A-K-Q-J-10 all of the same suit, is called a royal flush)
2. Four-of-a-kind
3. Full house (three cards of one rank, two of another)
4. Flush
5. Straight
6. Three-of-a-kind
7. Two pair
8. One pair
9. High card (a hand with no pair)

An ace is the highest-ranking card in the deck, but it also plays as the lowest card for straight purposes (A-2-3-4-5). Between two hands that would fit the same description above, rank is the determining factor; for example, a king-high flush beats a nine-high flush. If two players both have a pair of aces, then the next highest card in their hands determines the winner; for example, A-A-Q-5-4 beats A-A-J-10-5.

Here is an explanation of how a no-limit hold 'em hand plays out, divided into four stages.

Pre-Flop

The cards are dealt clockwise, beginning with the player seated to the left of the "dealer button." Each player at the table is dealt two cards, face down. These are known as the "hole cards."

The player immediately to the left of the dealer button must post the "small blind" and the player two seats to the left of the dealer button must post the "big blind." The big blind is double the amount of the small blind. For example, at the 25/50 blind level of a tournament, the small blind is forced to post 25 in chips and the big blind is forced to post 50 in chips.

The player immediately to the left of the big blind is first to act. That player's options are to:

(a) fold (throw the hole cards away and exit the hand);

(b) call (match the amount of the big blind);

(c) raise (bet any amount ranging from double the size of the big blind to all of the chips in the player's stack, also known as "moving all-in").

Moving clockwise around the table, all subsequent players have the same options: fold, call, or raise.

If no player raises, but at least one player calls the amount of the big blind, the player seated in the big blind has the option to "check," which means that he or she remains in the hand without committing any additional chips.

The "pre-flop" betting round concludes when either only

one player is still in the hand (and that player wins the pot) or all players remaining in the hand have committed the same amount of chips.

The Flop

Three "community cards" are dealt. All players at the table use these three cards, in combination with their two hole cards, to make a five-card poker hand.

Another betting round moves clockwise around the table, beginning on the left of the dealer button. The minimum amount that a player can bet is the value of the big blind.

All subsequent raises during this betting round must, at minimum, be equal to the size of the previous bet.

As in all betting rounds in no-limit hold 'em, the maximum amount that a player can bet is all of the chips in his or her stack.

The Turn

A fourth community card is dealt. All players now have six cards from which to make the best possible five-card hand. Another betting round follows the same rules and procedures as on the flop.

The River

A fifth and final community card is dealt. All players now have seven cards, of which they use exactly five to make the best possible hand. They can use both of their hole cards, one of their hole cards, or zero of their hole cards (known as "playing the board").

There is another betting round, using the same rules and procedures as on the flop and turn. At the conclusion of this betting round, all players still in the hand turn over their cards and the best five-card hand wins the pot.

If multiple players hold five-card hands of the same value—in other words, they tie for the best hand—they "chop" the pot, dividing it evenly among them.

At the conclusion of the hand, the dealer button moves one seat to the left.

About the Author

Though this is Eric Raskin's first book, he's no stranger to covering poker: He has been the editor-in-chief of *ALL IN* magazine and its website allinmag.com since 2005. He has been to the World Series of Poker five times as a member of the media, and though he has never bought into an actual WSOP event, he did eliminate Anthony Michael Hall on the very first hand of the WSOP media/celebrity charity tournament in 2006. He is also comfortably in the black as a small-stakes online-poker player.

Eric is a contributing writer to countless magazines and websites, including Grantland.com, *Playboy*, *ESPN The Magazine*, ESPN.com, and HBO.com. When he's not writing or editing poker articles, the majority of his work focuses on boxing. He is a six-time Boxing Writers Association of America award winner.

Eric lives in the Philadelphia suburbs with his wife Robin, daughter Olivia, son Eli, and beloved mystery mutt Rodney.

Other poker books by Huntington Press

Decide to Play Great Poker
by Annie Duke and John Vorhaus

Kill Everyone
by Lee Nelson, Tysen Streib, Steven Heston

Kill Phil
by Blair Rodman, Lee Nelson

Raiser's Edge
by Bertrand "ElkY" Grospellier, Lee Nelson,
Tysen Streib, and Tony Dunst

Telling Lies and Getting Paid
by Michael Konik

About Huntington Press

Huntington Press is a specialty publisher of Las Vegas-
and gambling-related books and periodicals.

Huntington Press
3665 Procyon Street
Las Vegas, Nevada 89103
702-252-0655